CREATIVE
HOME
DECOR
IN POLYMER
CLAY

SUE HEASER

NORTH LIGHT BOOKS
Cincinnati, Ohio
www.artistsnetwork.com

acknowledgments

I would firstly like to thank this little planet, which I have trotted round so much and found such wonder in its people, places, culture and history. This book, more than any other I have written, has been an outlet for that delight.

Thanks also to Polyform Products of Chicago for supplying the most of the clay used in this book—and for creating such wonderful clay in the first place!

And thanks to the North Light team, especially Jane, Christine and Maggie, whose enthusiasm and support made this book a joy to design and write.

dedication

To Taffy, tea & chocolate—
for their support

Library of Congress Cataloging-in-Publication Data

Heaser, Sue.
  Creative home decor in polymer clay / by Sue Heaser.
    p. cm.
  Includes bibliographical references and index.
    ISBN 1-58180-139-4 (alk. paper)
     1. Polymer clay craft. 2. House furnishings. I. Title.

TT297 .H42696 2001
731.4'2--dc21   2001042599

Editor: Jane Friedman
Designer: Andrea Short
Production coordinator: John Peavler
Layout artist: Kathy Gardner
Photographers: Christine Polomsky and Al Parrish
Stylist: Sharon Sweeney

about the author

Sue Heaser is an English polymer clay designer and artist who has worked full time in the medium since 1985. Initially she ran a small business making and supplying polymer clay jewelry to a large number of craft, fashion and gift outlets in eastern England. For the past six years she has been writing and illustrating articles and books on polymer clay, pushing the medium in ever-new directions.

After a globetrotting childhood in the Far East, Middle East and Africa, Sue studied at Art College and University in England. She initially worked for the Museum of London and progressed to a career as an archeological illustrator. She moved to rural eastern England with her husband when their first child was born and continued to combine motherhood (two daughters) with freelance illustration, glass engraving and puppetry. Then she discovered polymer clay, which has held her interest for longer than anything else to date! She works in jewelry, miniatures, dolls, puppets, mosaics, fine art, simulations and many other genres that are ever increasing in number.

Sue's first major book, *Making Polymer Clay Jewellery*, was published in June 1997. Three more books followed in quick succession: *Making Doll's House Miniatures in Polymer Clay*, *Making Miniature Dolls in Polymer Clay* and *The Polymer Clay Techniques Book*. Sue has also written dozens of polymer clay articles

〉 art nouveau frame > p. 84

for British and American magazines and several more books are in the pipeline.

In 1997, with the enthusiastic help of several others, she founded the British Polymer Clay Guild. She manages to combine her writing with an active role in the guild as well as teaching polymer clay classes all over the world.

Sue has many other interests. She plays the violin in a local orchestra, paints scenery for a drama group and spends every available moment of the summer sailing around the coasts of Britain and Europe. She is a qualified Yachtmaster Offshore. She has had two children's musicals published, which have been performed all over the world, and has also published *The Encyclopedia of Candlemaking* under the pen name of Sandie Lea. She lives in a beautiful part of rural England with her husband John and an assortment of pets.

) pearl veneer cutlery > p. 65

Living Room 22

Study 38

Dining Room 58

⟩ opaline lampshade > p. 30

) pearly polyclay pens and polyclay pencils > p. 50 and p. 55

introduction

Polymer clay is an extraordinary material: It is widely available, easy to use, and all you need to get started is one

2-ounce pack, your fingers, and a home oven! Most people start small by making a few beads, a model or a minia-

ture, and these are the traditional uses for polymer clay. But there is so much more that you can do with this won-

derful medium, and this book shows you how to make a collection of glorious items for your home.

> lemon beaded jug cover > p. 103

Today, polymer clay has established itself as an exciting and versatile craft material that is used by professionals and amateurs all over the world. It is more popular than it has ever been, and several manufacturers have responded by producing new and improved varieties of clay. Besides the gorgeous new color ranges, the new clays are softer in texture and stronger after baking. This gives artists the freedom to work larger and more inventively and opens up exciting possibilities for design—in particular with items for the home.

For example, preparing the new softer clays for a large project is now only a few minutes' work—gone are the painful regimes of kneading crumbling clay. Stronger clays mean that flimsy objects such as lampshades are robust and durable as well as beautiful. And the new colors have given us so many wonderful techniques and effects that we are spoilt for choice. There are also new products to complement the clays: I have used Liquid Sculpey in several projects in this book and it has added hugely to the box of polymer clay delights!

So whether you are trying polymer clay for the first time or have enjoyed it for years, here are projects to create beautiful artifacts for your home. I have suggested color schemes, but you can adapt any of the projects to match your home décor. The clays combine lusciously with fabric and cords for home furnishings, while metallic effect powders simulate antique bronze and gleaming silver. Many projects are inspired by objects of former times to bring a gracious sense of period living into your home. I hope you enjoy making the designs in this book and that many of your creations will become family heirlooms!

materials

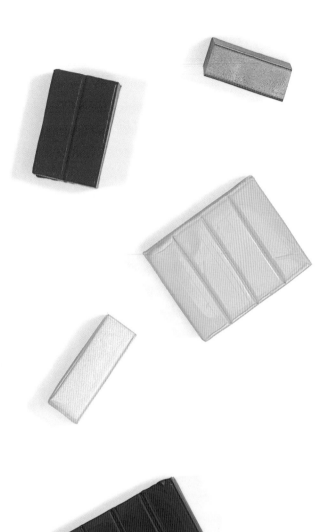

Polymer clay

I first came across polymer clay in the toy shop of our tiny town in the early 1980s. I took one look, saw that it was a modelling material that could be baked in an ordinary oven and carried some off with cries of glee! That enthusiasm has not diminished in all the intervening years, and polymer clay has surpassed all my wildest expectations of application and versatility. It is a truly remarkable material and is now used all over the world by artists and craftspeople, both professionals and amateurs, and in genres as diverse as fine art, illustration, jewelry, doll making and animation. If you have only just discovered it, you are in for a wonderful treat!

Polymer clay is available from art and craft stores all over the world. It is often known by its various brand names such as Sculpey and Fimo.

The clays vary among brands, and the following list gives the most widely available polymer clays and their properties. Most brands can be used for the projects in this book, apart from those that are brittle after baking. Note that some clays have a smoothable texture that allows joins in the clay to be smoothed over. This gives a good finish when making boxes or covering items.

>polymer clay qualities

))) Polymer clay is a colored modelling material and is a mixture of PVC particles, pigment and plasticizer.

))) It remains soft and pliable until it is hardened by baking in a domestic oven.

))) It is fine grained and malleable and allows highly detailed modelling.

))) Polymer clay normally comes in a wide range of colors that can be mixed to produce further colors.

))) If stored in cool conditions, it has a shelf life of several years.

))) It does not dry out and can be reused repeatedly until it is baked.

))) There is virtually no shrinkage or color change on baking.

))) The baked clay is durable and slightly flexible, although this varies among brands.

))) Once baked, it can be sanded, carved, sawn, painted and buffed to a shine.

))) Fresh clay can be added to hardened clay and then rebaked repeatedly.

))) It is nontoxic when used in accordance with manufacturers' instructions.

Sculpey clays

These are manufactured by Polyform Products of Chicago.

>Premo! Sculpey

This clay is ideal for making items for your home. It is extremely strong after baking and comes in a wonderful range of vivid colors that are named after artists' paint colors and mix remarkably true. The metallic and pearlescent clays are superb and can be used to give luscious effects. The clay is medium soft and it can be sliced thinly from the pack and fed straight into a pasta machine to avoid any hand kneading. For this reason it is ideal for projects that require large amounts of clay. Most of the projects in this book were made using Premo! The clay is smoothable.

>Sculpey III

Softer than Premo! Sculpey, Sculpey III can be used straight from the pack. It has an excellent color range, but since it is relatively fragile after baking, it is not recommended for larger projects that require strength or for detailed work with fine modelling techniques. It is smoothable.

>Transparent Liquid Sculpey

This is a liquid polymer clay that can be tinted with oil paints and used in dozens of different ways. It remains a syrupy liquid until it is baked at the same temperature as regular polymer clay. It can simulate delicate enamel effects, stained glass and ceramic glazes and is a useful grout for polymer clay mosaics. It can be used as a strong adhesive to attach fresh clay to baked clay and to fill cracks. Artists are still finding exciting new applications for this wonderful material!

>Granitex

A stone-effect clay that has tiny fibers mixed into it and comes in a range of subtle colors. It has similar properties to Sculpey III and is quite brittle after baking.

Fimo clays

Fimo is manufactured by Eberhard Faber in Germany. It is one of the best-known polymer clays and is available all over the world.

>Fimo Classic

This is the original Fimo that has been available for many years. Today Fimo Classic is somewhat softer than the original version and comes in fewer colors. Fimo requires kneading before use until it is uniformly soft and malleable. It tends to crumble at first but soon softens into a usable texture. The baked clay is strong and it is a good choice for larger items for the home. It is partly smoothable.

>Fimo Soft

This clay now has the larger color range of the Fimo clays. The clay is softer than Fimo Classic, although it seems to harden in the pack after opening. The baked clay is not as strong as Fimo Classic. The range includes transparent colored clays, stone-effect clays, metallic clays and fluorescent clays. It is smoothable.

Cernit

Manufactured in Germany, Cernit is of a different consistency than most other clays. The colors have a slight translucency or porcelain effect, and the clay is not smoothable. It is initially fairly firm but softens as you knead. Hand heat can make the clay quite limp as you work, so allow it to rest if this happens. The baked clay is extremely strong.

Creall-Therm

This clay is manufactured in the Netherlands. It is a medium firm clay that requires some kneading before use. Although it comes in many beautiful colors, it lacks some of the more brilliant pigments and metallics. The baked clay is very strong, but care should be taken to bake thoroughly or the clay does not reach full strength. It is smoothable.

Du-Kit

Manufactured in New Zealand, Du-Kit is a medium firm clay and good for detail. It is extremely strong after baking and it is smoothable.

Modelene

An Australian polymer clay, Modelene has similar properties to Cernit. It is extremely strong after baking and not smoothable.

Modello/Formello

This is another German clay that is sold under both the above names. It is quite a firm clay. It is not very strong after baking and is not smoothable.

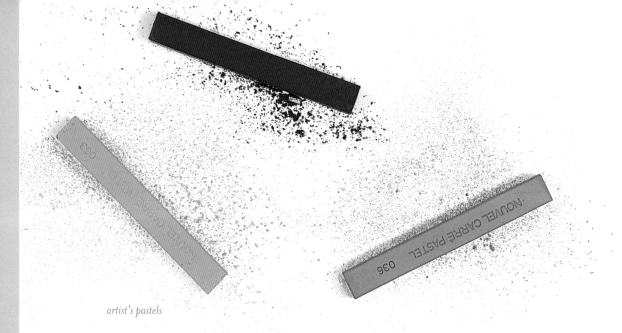

artist's pastels

Clay softeners

Several manufacturers produce softeners that can be added to the clay. Fimo Mix Quick is a very soft base-colored clay and Sculpey Diluent is a liquid softener.

Storing clay

Polymer clay has a shelf life of several years, although the clay will slowly become firmer as time passes. I have ten-year-old clay that is still perfectly usable, with a bit of effort!

Store your opened clay in an airtight container to keep dust out, and keep it in a cool, dark place—a sunny windowsill will soon partly bake your clay and ruin it.

Polymer clay can damage some plastics, so do not store it in plastic containers unless you line them with baking parchment, polythene or foil. Clay can be stored in polythene bags, but avoid paper because this will leach out the plasticizer and dry out the clay.

Other materials

One of the most exciting aspects of polymer clay is that it can be used in combination with many other art and craft materials. However, you must take care that the materials are compatible with polymer clay. The wrong type of paint, for example, will never dry properly on polymer clay, and some problems do not show up until a few months after the item has been made. All the following materials are known to be compatible and I have tested them myself over many years.

>powders

Metallic and mica powders produce some of the most brilliant effects on polymer clay, and if you have never tried them, you have a wonderful surprise in store! The most startling effects are obtained when you brush the powders onto soft, black clay, but it is fun to experiment with different colored clays as well. The clay is then baked and given a coating of varnish to protect the powder. Metallic and mica powders are available from art and craft suppliers, and some clay manufacturers produce their own versions. Pearl Ex powders are mica-based and particularly recommended. Avoid breathing the dust when using any of these powders.

I do not advise using cosmetic powders because some of these may discolor in time.

>artist's soft pastels

These are very useful for soft, graded effects on white or light-colored polymer clay. Rub a little pastel onto some paper, and use a paintbrush to scoop up some powder and brush it onto the soft clay before baking.

>metal leaf

Gold and silver leaf can be applied to soft clay for wonderful metallic effects. Use the imitation leaf rather than the real thing, which costs a small fortune! You need to varnish over the imitation leaf to prevent tarnishing. Leaf is also available in copper and variegated colors.

>paint

Baked polymer clay can be painted with acrylic paints. Do not use enamel or solvent-based paints because these never dry properly on polymer clay. Before painting polymer clay, brush over the surface with denatured alcohol (methylated spirits) to de-grease it or the acrylic paint will not stick. Paint may bleed on some clays after time; to prevent this, apply a coat of matte varnish to the clay before painting.

>epoxy enamel

This is a two-part epoxy resin that can be used to give lovely transparent enamel effects on

powders

polymer clay. It is sold under various brand names such as Envirotex Lite and Crystal Sheen. Since it is normally used as a deep gloss coating for wood, it can usually be found in hardware and craft materials stores. Check that the instructions require you to mix together two different liquids—that is the kind of product you need because it sets to a glasslike finish and can be poured up to a depth of about ⅛" (3mm). Enamel paints are not the same. Jewelry and craft materials suppliers also sell a version that is precolored and sold as epoxy enamels (cold enamels in Europe).

You can buy special colors, either opaque or transparent, for tinting the enamel, but I have had good results with ordinary oil paint as well.

>varnish

It is not necessary to varnish baked polymer clay unless you need to protect powders or paint or you need a shiny surface.

The various manufacturers produce both gloss and matt varnish that vary in durability. I prefer the Fimo matte and gloss spirit (alcohol) based varnishes, which are extremely durable.

Future floor polish, made by Johnson & Johnson, is actually an acrylic varnish and is a cheap and durable alternative to proprietary varnishes. It is called Johnson's Klear in Europe. Flecto Varathane is another brand that is recommended for polymer clay.

As with paint, never use solvent-based varnish on polymer clay, or even acrylic varnish in an aerosol can. Neither will dry properly on the clay.

>glues

Polymer clay can be tricky to glue—some glues just do not work! Choose one of the following:

- superglue (cyanoacrylate glue) — for gluing together baked clay pieces and for gluing baked clay to anything hard such as metal or glass for a strong bond.
- epoxy glue — as above, but less convenient as it takes longer to set. The bond, however, will be even stronger.
- PVA glue such as Tacky Glue or Sobo — for gluing baked polymer clay to paper, card and fabric. A thin smear applied to baked clay, glass or ceramic will help fresh clay adhere.
- Liquid Sculpey — this can be used sparingly to attach unbaked clay to baked clay and to repair broken pieces, but it has very low tack until it is baked. After baking, it is extremely strong

gold leaf

Tools

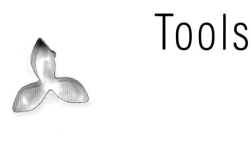

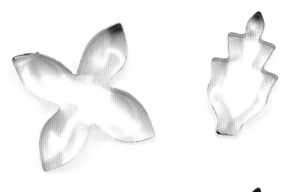

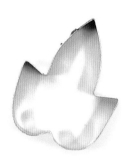

cutters

ceramic tiles

Polymer clay is a very beginner-friendly material because virtually everything you need to get started is probably already in your home. As you become more advanced with this fascinating material, you may find that you will want to add more gadgets to your toolbox. However, this is not essential. After nearly two decades of working with the clays, my own toolbox still has only a small selection of simple, everyday items!

This list gives the basic tools and equipment that you will need for the projects in this book. Other tools are listed under specific projects.

Work surface

You will need a smooth work surface that you can wipe clean. A melamine tablemat, a sheet of toughened glass or a large ceramic tile are all ideal. Avoid surfaces that are textured.

Craft knife

This is the second essential item. Choose one with a curved blade as shown in the photograph and you will have a cutting knife combined with an appliqué tool for delicate work.

Blades

Tissue blades are widely available from polymer clay suppliers. They are ideal for slicing millefiori canes and blocks of clay and for cutting straight lines on clay sheets.

Rollers & pasta machines

You will often need to roll clay into sheets. A pasta machine is a wonderful tool for this and will also help you knead your clay and mix colors. Alternatively, you can use an acrylic roller, a glass bottle or a smooth rolling pin. If you place two strips of thick card or wood on either side of the clay as you roll, the sheets will be kept to a uniform thickness.

Assorted tools

You will need a collection of piercing and small sculpting tools. My favorites are
- a large, blunt tapestry needle
- the dried out refill of a ball point pen with a cone-shaped tip

craft knife and tissue blade

- glass ball-headed pins—I use the glass ball end
- a large darning needle for piercing beads

You can set pins and needles in clay handles and bake them, but I prefer to leave the eye of a needle exposed—it is a useful decorating tool!

Cutters

A wonderful variety of different shaped cutters are available for polymer clay. Kemper cutters are particularly good with plungers to push out the clay after cutting. They come in a wide range of sizes and shapes. You can also use cookie cutters, cutters made for gum paste (sugarcraft) cake decoration and improvised cutters. I have a collection of brush protectors that come free when you buy an artist's paintbrush, and these are perfect as small round cutters.

Stamps

Rubber stamps are great fun to use on polymer clay. Choose stamps that have clear and deeply cut images for the best results. Always brush the clay surface with talcum powder before stamping to prevent sticking. Several of the projects in this book show you how to make your own stamps out of polymer clay.

Baking equipment

A simple cookie sheet lined with baking parchment or plain paper is all you need for baking polymer clay. Many of the projects in this book are baked on ceramic tiles so that you can create the item on the tile and then transfer it to the oven without having to move it.

!! equipment safety

If you "borrow" kitchen equipment to use for polymer clay, do not use the items for food as well unless they can be thoroughly washed and have no crevices to trap the clay. The clay is nontoxic, but you should still avoid eating it!

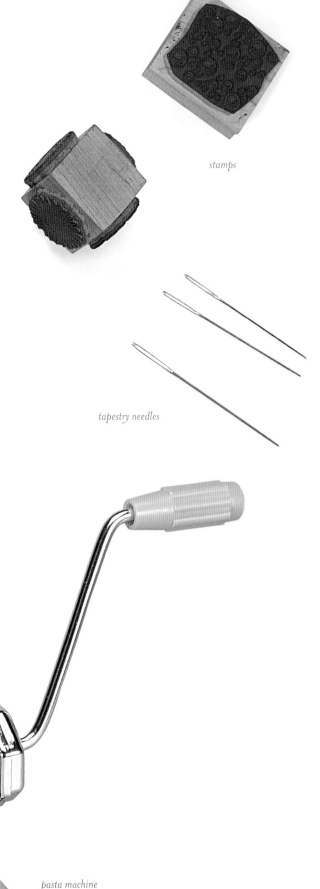

stamps

tapestry needles

pasta machine

Techniques

Basic polymer clay techniques are quick and easy to learn. Most of us have learned simple clay modelling as a child. However, there is no limit to how far you can progress with polymer clay, and most people find that they rapidly develop their skills toward more exciting and advanced techniques. Try to keep a light touch, and be constantly aware of the importance of a good finish. Fingernail nicks and uneven pieces will never allow you to achieve real excellence in your work.

Preparing the clay

You should normally knead the clay until it is uniformly smooth and soft before use, although clay cut straight from the block is used for some projects such as mosaics. It is not necessary to condition clay for lengthy periods. It will actually weaken the clay if you mix too long and incorporate too much air. Some clays require more kneading than others. A good guide is to knead until a ⅜" (10mm) thick log of soft clay will bend into a U without cracking.

To knead your clay, cut off a piece and roll it between your hands into a log, fold the log in half and roll again. Continue rolling and folding until the clay is uniformly soft and malleable. Larger quantities can be kneaded in small amounts and then combined.

Softer clays can be kneaded straight from the pack with a pasta machine, a great advantage when using larger quantities of clay.

Kneading clay with a pasta machine

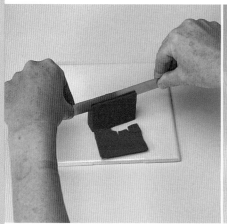 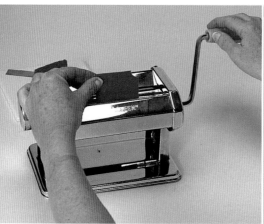 

1 Unwrap a block of clay and stand it on its side. Use a blade to cut thin slices straight from the block. The slices should be about the same thickness as the thickest setting on your pasta machine to avoid straining the machine.

2 Roll each slice through the pasta machine, and it will flatten into a sheet. Press the sheets together in pairs and roll again, continuing until you have one large sheet. Fold the sheet in half and pass through again. You will need to pass the clay through the machine about six to ten times to thoroughly knead it, depending on the softness of the clay.

3 When you have folded a sheet of clay, make sure that you place the fold to the side as you pass it through the pasta machine. This will ensure that any air bubbles are squeezed out and not trapped in the clay. If you do get air bubbles, always fold them to the outside and they will disappear with repeated rollings.

Making logs and balls

These are the basic shapes that you will need to make repeatedly when working with polymer clay. They are also the starting point for many projects.

>*forming logs*

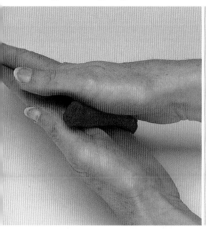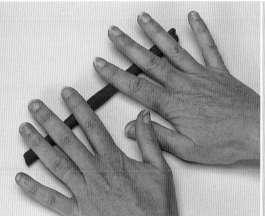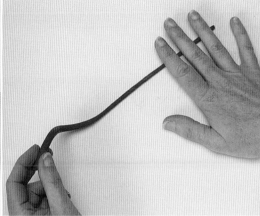

1 Squeeze the kneaded clay roughly into a log shape in your hands and then roll it back and forth between your palms. This will smooth and lengthen the log.

2 Lay the log on your work surface and roll it back and forth with your fingers spread out lightly over it. You need to keep your fingers moving constantly from side to side along the length of the log to prevent any thin areas developing. Roll lightly, or you will squash some areas and the log will not be even. With practice, you will be able to make long and even logs of any thickness.

3 Some projects require very fine logs of 1/16" (1.5mm) thick or less. First make a 1/4" (6mm) thick log. Hold one end in one hand and use the other to roll out the other end, thinning it as you roll. Keep your hand moving back and forth as before. The thicker part will provide a handle for controlling the thin part so you do not have to touch the thin thread of clay once it is formed.

))) adjusting the *clay texture*

If your purchased clay is too hard or too soft, you can alter the consistency with the following techniques.

Leaching

This is useful if you have clay that is too soft. Roll the clay into a sheet and press this between two pieces of ordinary white paper. Leave for several hours or overnight and the paper will absorb some of the plasticizer to leave the clay much firmer.

Softening

Knead the clay with a proprietary clay softener such as Fimo Mix Quick or Sculpey Diluent following the instructions on the pack. Very old, hard clay can often be brought back to a usable consistency by chopping it into small pieces and crushing it with a large rolling pin. Add a softening agent and continue rolling and mixing until it is smooth. I do not advise that you add mineral oil or other oils: Polymer clay is a chemical mix and I personally do not feel it is safe to complicate the chemical soup. Use the softeners provided by the manufacturers—they are not expensive.

>*forming balls*

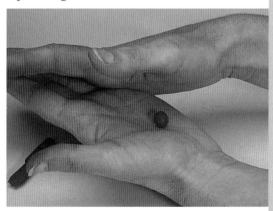

Place a piece of clay between your palms and, holding the lower hand still, apply light pressure with your upper hand, rotating it in small circles. Open your hands to see how round the ball has become and continue as necessary, until you find the right amount of pressure to form a perfect ball.

Rolling sheets

If you do not have a pasta machine for rolling sheets, lay some kneaded clay on your work surface and roll firmly with a roller or strong bottle. To ensure that the sheet is of even thickness, place strips of wood on either side of the clay as you roll for the roller ends to rest on as the sheet thins.

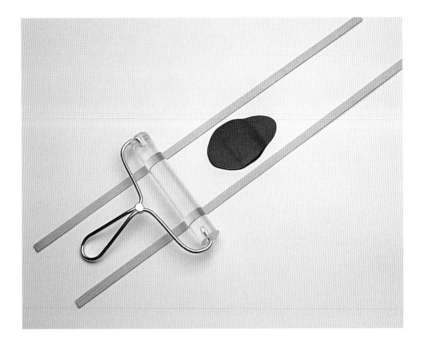

Colors

All the main brands of polymer clay come in a large range of colors that can be mixed together to make even more colors. In fact, you only need a few basic colors to mix a useful palette of your own, although the brilliance of the mixtures will vary between brands.

The following list gives the basic range of colors needed for the projects in this book and suggestions on how to mix them if necessary. All the different brands have different names for their colors, so I use simple descriptive names here so that you can identify the colors in the brand that you are using.

Mixtures are suggestions only because the intensity of pigments varies considerably between brands. You can mix a light version of any color by adding a little of the color to white or translucent. Always mix a small quantity first to check the proportions you need of each color.

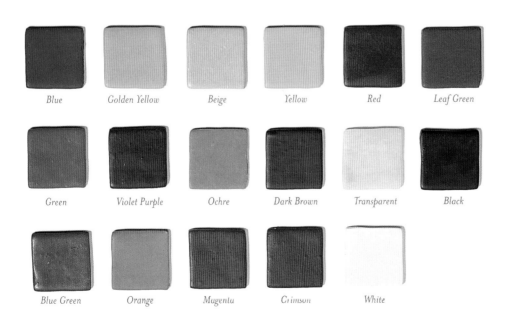

Blue	Golden Yellow	Beige	Yellow	Red	Leaf Green
Green	Violet Purple	Ochre	Dark Brown	Transparent	Black
Blue Green	Orange	Magenta	Crimson	White	

mixtures>

⟩ Orange = 3 parts yellow + 1 part red

⟩ Golden Yellow = yellow + trace of red

⟩ Leaf Green = 2 parts green + 1 part brown

⟩ Blue-Green = equal parts of blue + green

⟩ Ochre = dark brown + yellow + white

⟩ Beige = white + trace of brown
   ** This is "Ecru" in Premo! Sculpey

Color mixing

Mixtures in this book are usually given as to how many parts of each color to mix. The following example shows how to mix orange.

>mixture: orange = 1 part red + 3 parts yellow

 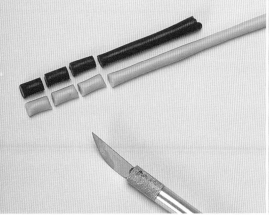 

1 To measure equal parts, first roll one color into a log and cut several equal lengths, using a ruler to guide you.

2 Repeat with the second color (and a third if necessary), making sure that the logs are the same thickness and the cut lengths are all identical in size.

3 Now combine the lengths according to the number of parts given in the mixture recipe. Roll the two colors together into a log, fold the log in half and roll again, repeating several times. At first the clay will become streaky, then the colors will combine to make the new color. You can also mix clays with the pasta machine, folding and rerolling the sheet until the new color is thoroughly mixed.

tip

pearlescent colors

Several brands have pearl and metallic colors. I have used Premo! Sculpey metallics and pearls in the projects because they provide such a brilliant shine, but you could use another brand, although the effect will not be quite the same. To create an optimum shiny surface when using these colors, you need to roll the clay into a sheet, fold and roll again several times to eliminate all streakiness.

Marbling

This is easily done and is only the intermediate stage of mixing two or more colored clays together; however, it needs care to do it well. You will not get a streaky marble result by mixing with a pasta machine, so it must be done by hand.

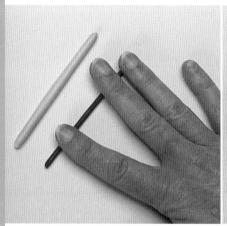

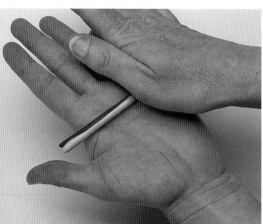

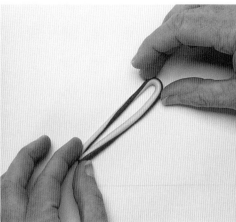

1 Roll the colors to be marbled into equal length logs. Depending on the proportions, they may not be the same thickness.

2 Press the two logs together and roll them in your hands until they have doubled in length.

3 Fold the log in half, being careful not to twist it. You want the two colors visible in straight lines all along the length.

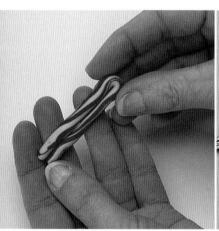

4 Roll again and fold again in the same way, continuing until the lines of color are thin stripes. If you are going to roll the log into a marbled sheet, you will need to continue until the lines are very thin because they will spread when they are rolled flat.

5 This shows the effects of hand marbling. Strong contrasting colors look most effective. The right hand logs are marbled dark brown and gold, which give a lovely faux wood effect when rolled flat.

Baking

Take care when baking your polymer clay creations; it is heartbreaking to ruin a piece at this point! Follow these guidelines and always bake a test piece first if you are unsure.

•Most polymer clays should be baked in an ordinary home oven at 275°F (130°C) for 20 to 30 minutes, but check the pack first.

•Bake pieces on a cookie sheet that has been covered with baking parchment or paper to prevent shiny marks appearing where the clay rests. Foil can be used to support thin items that might sag as they heat up.

•Ceramic tiles are useful for baking because you can create and bake on the tile without moving the object. If you are baking on a tile, you will need to bake for at least 10 minutes longer.

•All the clays have a nontoxic rating and will not cause harm when used in your kitchen oven. If you are baking in quantity on a regular basis, you may prefer to bake the clay inside a deep baking pan sealed with foil or use a dedicated toaster oven. This will keep clay smells away from the family dinner!

•Oven thermostats can vary in accuracy. The best way to test your oven for clay is to bake some test strips of clay, 1/16" (1.5mm) thick and about 2" (5cm) long. Allow these to cool and bend them in half. If you are using a strong clay such as Premo! or Fimo Classic, you should be able to bend the clay into a U several times before it cracks. If it cracks easily, try a 10° higher oven temperature. If the clay scorches, turn the oven down 10° and test again.

Sanding and buffing

After baking, polymer clay can be sanded with fine-grade wet and dry sandpaper to smooth the surface. Hold the clay under a gently running water and sand with sandpaper grades between 600 and 800.

After sanding, you can buff the surface to a shine with a piece of stiff fabric or quilt batting.

Safety

All brands of polymer clay have nontoxic labeling and are very safe compared to some pottery and art materials. However, it is wise to follow simple precautions with any craft material. The following are recommended for polymer clay:

•Always wash your hands after using the clays.

•Do not use polymer clay tools and utensils for food and do not allow baked or unbaked polymer clay to come into contact with food.

•Follow manufacturers' instructions as to baking temperatures.

•If polymer clay accidentally burns, avoid breathing the fumes and ventilate the room thoroughly.

! warning

Never allow polymer clay to burn. A toxic gas is produced that will smell terrible and warn you immediately that something is wrong. If this happens, turn off the oven, open the windows and leave the room until the smell has gone. You will not be harmed if you do this—the smell is too horrid for you to manage to inhale enough to harm yourself!

baking sheet

Millefiori canes

This is a popular polymer clay technique and gets its name from a similar effect in glass-making. Logs of different thicknesses are combined into a single log to build an image in cross-section rather like holiday candy or seaside rock. The "cane," as it is called, is then pulled or rolled longer to make the image smaller. Slices can then be taken from the log and applied to sheets of clay or used to cover ceramic or glass items. Two simple examples are given here so that you can use the technique as a variation for some of the projects in this book. Boxes and frames, cutlery and vases are all suitable for covering with cane slices to make beautiful items for your home.

>moon and star cane

>sun cane

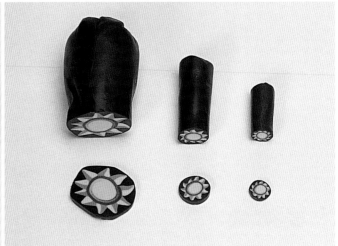

Form a ¼" (6mm) thick log of white clay, about 12" (30cm) long, and squeeze it into a triangular cross section all along its length. Cut it into five lengths for the five points of the star. Arrange these around a round ¼" (6mm) thick log. Form five more triangular section logs in purple clay to fill the spaces between the white points. Roll the cane thinner to reduce it and cut a 2" (5cm) length. Wrap this in a sheet of purple clay. Press a thick sheet of white clay onto one side of the cane for the moon, pinching the ends into points. Wrap again in purple clay. Roll the log thinner again to reduce the image.

This cane is made in a similar way to the star cane above. Form a ½" (12mm) thick log of yellow clay and wrap it in a sheet of red for the sun's center. The sun's rays are made like the star's points, only each ray is two colored logs, orange and yellow, pressed together before shaping. From this make ten ¼" (6mm) thick triangular logs, each 2" (5cm) long, and press them around the center log. Fill in the spaces between the rays with triangular black logs and wrap the whole in a black sheet. Reduce and then slice.

Examples of millefiori projects

Simple rosebud cane slices decorate a dainty needlework set. The pincushion is made using the base of a baby food jar as the former and a stuffed pad of green silk is glued inside to hold the pins. The needle case is made using a glass test tube for a former while the thimble is simply covered in white clay, leaving the working end protruding. See page 81 for instructions on making boxes with formers.

The frame is made in the same way as the Art Nouveau Frame on page 84. After baking, moon and stars cane slices are applied and the frame is rebaked.

The box is made in the same way as the Trinket Box on page 80. Sun cane slices are applied to the baked box using a dab of PVA glue or Liquid Sculpey to help them adhere. The box is then rebaked.

the *living* **room**

))) **THIS IS THE ROOM IN** *our house where I love to relax. The chairs are cushioned and cradling, while drapes and carpets are in peaceful, toning colors. In winter, a wood-burning stove makes the dark evenings cozy, while table lamps shine pools of light onto your hands when you read or sew. In summer, the south-facing patio doors can stand open to bring the fragrance of the garden into the house and the room is full of sunshine.*

THE PROJECTS IN THIS *chapter show you how to create beautiful artifacts for your own living room. Color is important in home décor and while the subtle colors of the Arabian Palace clock would please in virtually any setting, any project could easily be altered to fit your existing décor. For example, the copper and gold tassels would look wonderful made in blue and silver for a dark velvet curtain, while the brilliant flame-colored lampshade can be transformed into another mood by using pastels such as the palest lavender or a creamy rose.*

Tassel Tiebacks

Tassels have a long, aristocratic history and are used in cultures all over the world. Traditional tassels are time-consuming to make, but this polymer clay version is quick and easy. Tassels have many uses in the home, and here they make opulent tiebacks for your living room curtains. Once you have mastered the basic technique, you will be able to make all kinds of tassels to decorate your home.

materials>

> 2-ounce (60g) blocks of polymer clay: 1 copper and 1 gold, plus scrap clay for the formers

> foil

> teaspoon

> knitting needle

> artist's paintbrush handle or similar tool for grooving

> yarn for the tassel skirt (I used a thick terra-cotta chenille yarn)

> matching cord, about ⅛" (3mm) thick

> tacky glue

> stiff cardstock for making the tassel skirts

> scissors

> paperclip

> roller

> craft knife

> tile (optional)

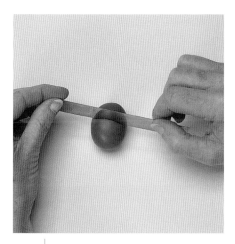

one | Make the tassel formers

Form a 1½" (4cm) ball of scrap clay and roll it between your hands to make an oval about 1¼" (3cm) diameter and 2" (5cm) long. Bake the oval for 30 minutes. Allow it to cool until you can handle it but it is still warm. With a sharp blade, cut neatly through the "equator" of the oval to give two identical formers. (Clay is much easier to cut when it is still warm.)

two | Wrap formers in foil

Wrap each former tightly in foil, folding the edges of the foil onto the flat end of the former and trimming away any excess foil.

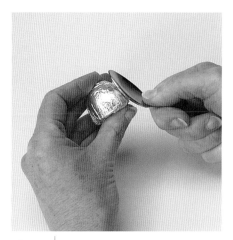

three | Smooth the surface

Use the back of a teaspoon to press the foil firmly onto the former and smooth out any wrinkles. A smooth surface will make it easier to remove the former from the clay after baking.

four | Make the tassel cups

Roll out a sheet of copper clay, about ⅟₁₆" (1.5mm) thick, rolling and folding it several times so that the sheen on the surface is smooth and continuous. Cut out a rough shape, about 6" (15cm) square, and wrap this around the domed part of one of the formers. Trim the clay to size so that the ends meet neatly and butt together.

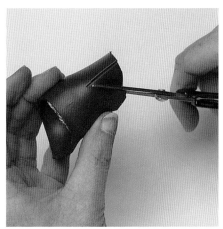

five | Cut notches

Cut V-notches out of the clay at the top of the former's dome so that the sheet can be pressed flat and dovetailed together rather like fitting orange peel back onto an orange.

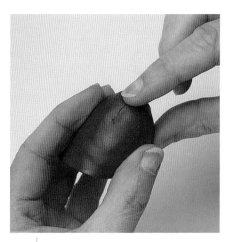

six | Rejoin and smooth

Press the clay down, trimming further if necessary. Smooth the joins with the tip of your finger, smearing the surface of the clay slightly to make a continuous shiny surface.

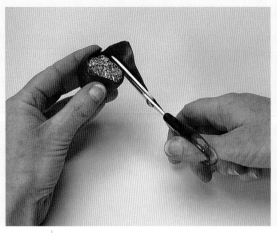

seven | Trim excess clay

Trim away the excess clay around the base of the former with scissors and neaten the bottom edge. Take care that the clay does not curve around onto the bottom of the former, or the tassel cup will be difficult to remove from the former after baking. Repeat steps 4 to 7 to cover the second former.

eight | Decorate the tassel cups

Form a long, thin log of gold clay, about ⅛" (3mm) thick and 12" (30cm) long. Cut this in half and lay the two pieces together. Now twist the lengths into a rope by twisting the right-hand end away from you and the left-hand end toward you. Coax the clay to twist all along the length, keeping the twists as even as possible.

nine | Add the first rope

Wrap the rope around the base of the tassel cup, pressing it onto the edge of the copper clay so that it is attached all around.

ten | Add the second rope

Wrap a second rope around just above the first. For each rope, trim the ends where they meet and butt the two ends together neatly.

eleven | Add the ball

Form a ⅝" (15mm) ball of copper clay and press this onto the top of the tassel. It will flatten slightly as you press to make an attractive finial.

twleve | Pierce the ball

Use the knitting needle to pierce a hole right through the ball and the clay sheet covering of the former. Rotate the needle to enlarge the hole, which needs to be ³⁄₁₆" (5mm) wide, or at least wide enough for your chosen cord to pass through.

thirteen | Make the leaves

Form a ¼" (6mm) thick log of gold clay and cut six ¼" (6mm) lengths. Roll these into balls and shape each into a teardrop. Press each teardrop down onto a tile so that it thins and forms a leaf shape. Use your knife to mark veins.

fourteen | Add the leaves

Slide your knife blade under each leaf to lift it off the tile, and press the leaves around the top of the tassel cup, just below the ball. Space them evenly and give each a little twist to make it look more natural.

fifteen | Add a thin log

Form a thin log of gold clay, about ¹⁄₁₆" (1.5mm) thick, and wrap this around the tassel cup between the leaves and the ball finial. Repeat steps 8 to 15 for the second cup.

sixteen | Make the tube bead

Form a 1¼" (3cm) ball of copper clay and roll it on the tile to shape it into a cylinder, 1½" (4cm) long and about ⅞" (22mm) wide. Stand it on one end, and use the knitting needle to pierce down through the bead, then push the bead right onto the needle.

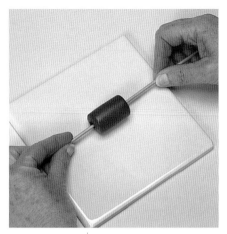

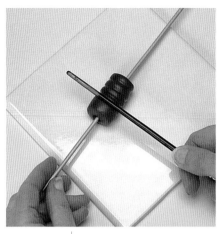

seventeen | Enlarge hole

Now grasp the needle in your hands, one on either side of the bead, and roll the bead back and forth on the tile. This will enlarge the hole and smooth the sides of the bead. The hole needs to be about ¼" (6mm) wide, or wide enough for three thicknesses of your cord to fit through fairly tightly.

eighteen | Groove the clay

With the bead still on the knitting needle, hold a paintbrush handle across the bead and, pressing down lightly, roll the bead back and forth on the tile so that the handle "grooves" the clay. Repeat to make five evenly spaced grooves.

nineteen | Add ropes

Make some more gold clay rope as in step 8, and wrap lengths around the center and the two end grooves on the bead.

Bake the bead with the tassel cups for at least 30 minutes. Allow to cool, then ease the tassel cups off the formers. You may find this easier to do if you open out the foil at the base of each former so that you can ease the former out of the foil first, then pull the foil out of the cup.

twenty | Make the tassel skirt

Cut a piece of stiff card into a 6" (15cm) square. Wind the yarn around this until you have a good thick hank for the tassel skirt.

twenty-one | Cut off hank

Cut through the yarn along the bottom edge with sharp scissors—this releases the yarn from the card and gives you a hank of 12" (30cm) lengths of yarn. Repeat for the second tassel skirt.

twenty-two | Add cord

Cut a length of cord that is long enough to go round your curtain twice and add an extra 18" (45cm). If the cord starts to fray, glue the ends together with a little tacky glue. Bend a paperclip into a hook and use this to pull one end of the cord through one of the tassel cups.

twenty-three | Tie together

Spread out flat one of the hanks of yarn and lay the end of the cord along the center. Use a piece of yarn to tie a tight knot around the halfway point of the hank, trapping the end of the cord. As you tighten the knot, the yarn will gather together into the tassel skirt.

twenty-four | Add tassel cup

Hold the tassel by the cord and pull the yarn down over and around the knot. Arrange the yarn so that the cord emerges from the center of the gathered yarn. Pull the other end of the cord to draw the tassel into the tassel cup.

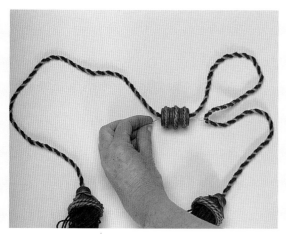

twenty-five | Assemble the tieback

Thread the second end of the cord through the tube bead and then through the second tassel cup. Attach the second tassel skirt in the same way as the first. Lay the tassels out in front of you and push the paperclip hook through the tube bead. Catch a loop of cord from about halfway along and pull it through the tube bead. This almost magically gives you the two loops for the tieback and leaves the two tassels dangling by their cords.

twenty-six | Create loops

Pull the loops through the tube bead to make them the same length and arrange the tassels to hang one just above the other. Hang one loop over the hook on your wall behind the curtain, pass the tieback around the front of the curtain and hang the other loop over the same hook. Make another tieback in the same way for a matching pair of curtains.

>*project two* Opaline Lampshade

Tinted translucent polymer clay is an excellent material for lampshades, and here it simulates opaline colored glass or translucent shell. A wire lampshade frame is used to support the luscious fire-colored sheets of marbled and baked clay. Use strong clay for this project such as Premo! Sculpey, which is flexible when baked.

Lampshade frames are available in all shapes and sizes. The one used in this project has eight sections and is 9½" (24cm) tall and 14½" (37cm) diameter across the bottom. Choose a frame that has fairly straight sections so that you do not have to bend the baked clay sheets too much.

materials>

⟩ 2-ounce (60g) blocks of polymer clay: 4 translucent, 1 golden yellow, 1 magenta, 1 red and 2 black (*⁎ NOTE: These quantities are for the lampshade given above. You may need to adjust the quantities depending on the size of your chosen frame.*)

⟩ wire lampshade frame with the sides divided into six to eight sections

⟩ plain sheet of paper, pencil and scissors

⟩ large cookie sheet lined with baking parchment

⟩ superglue

⟩ scrap clay for making the stamp

⟩ charm or small piece of jewelry for the stamp

⟩ talcum powder

⟩ Super Bronze Pearl Ex powder

⟩ gloss varnish

⟩ roller

⟩ tile (optional)

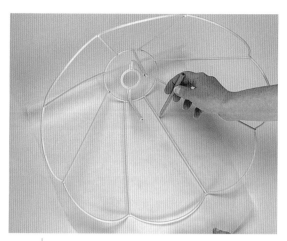

one | Make the template

Lay the lampshade on the paper and draw around the outside of one of the sections to make a template. Cut out the shape.

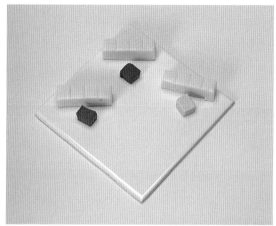

two | Measure out clay

Divide one of the blocks of translucent into three equal pieces. Each one of these will be tinted a different color. Take $\frac{1}{16}$ of a block of red clay and marble this into one of the translucent pieces to make longitudinal streaks (see page 18). Repeat with the yellow and magenta clays.

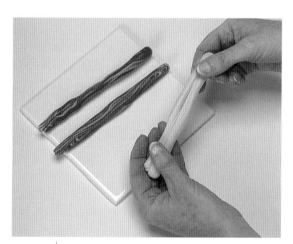

three | Form marbled logs

The marbled logs should look like this. The streaks are still visible and they are now ready to be turned into a marble sheet.

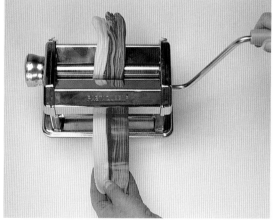

four | Create marbled sheets

Press the three logs together side by side with the red in the center. Flatten them in your hands and then feed them through the widest setting on the pasta machine, end first, so that they form a sheet of clay with longitudinal streaks. Pass them through again, in the same direction, at a medium setting of about $\frac{1}{16}$" (1.5mm) thick.

five | Thin the sheets

Fold the sheet in half and pass through the pasta machine again. This will begin to blend the clay and merge the colors where they join. Repeat several more times, folding and passing the clay through the machine longitudinally until you are happy with the result. Finally, roll the clay through on the thinnest setting that your machine can handle without rumpling the clay. (If you are unsure of this, test with scrap clay first.)

six | Make the panels

Cut the sheet in half across its middle and lay the two pieces side by side on a paper-covered surface so that the clay does not stick. Flip one of the sheets so that the two magenta stripes are placed together. Overlap the join slightly and press all along it to seal the pieces into one sheet. Now lay the paper template centrally over the sheet and cut out the panel shape. Save all the scraps as you can marble them into the next sheet.

seven | Repeat and bake

Repeat to make as many panels as your lampshade frame requires. Transfer the panels to a cookie sheet lined with baking parchment. Bake for 30 minutes to be sure that the clay is fully baked and strong.

eight | Attach the panels

Run a thin line of superglue around the edge of a frame section. Press on a clay panel, bending it to fit any curves and using scissors to trim the clay if necessary. Continue around the frame, making sure that all the edges are glued down firmly.

nine | Make "metal" trimmings

Form a thick rope of black clay by twisting together two logs about ³⁄₁₆" (5mm) thick (see page 26). Lay the panel template on the cookie sheet and curve the rope around the base, trimming the ends to fit. Make as many curved ropes as your lampshade has panels.

  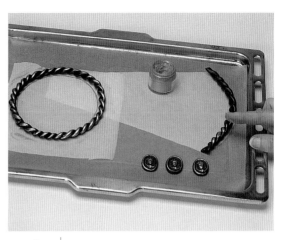

ten | Make a stamp

To make a stamp, knead a small ball of scrap clay and flatten it onto a tile. Brush the surface with talcum powder to prevent sticking, and press a small piece of jewelry firmly onto the clay surface. Remove the jewelry and bake the stamp for 20 to 30 minutes.

eleven | Create medallions

Form some small balls of black clay, shape each to match the shape of your stamp and press down onto the tile. Brush with talc and then impress each on with the stamp.

twelve | Make top ring

To make the top ring, turn the lampshade upside-down on a piece of paper and draw around the top to make a template. Form a black rope of clay in the same way as in step 9 and curve it around this template. Trim the ends and butt them together. Dip your finger into the bronze powder and brush over the surface of all the black clay pieces. Only the raised areas will be coated with bronze to give the appearance of rich antique metal!

thirteen | Bake

Bake all the black pieces for 30 minutes. When cool, coat with gloss varnish to protect the powder.

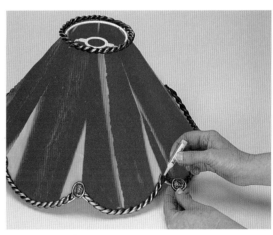

fourteen | Attach trimmings

Use superglue to stick the "metal" ropes around the bottom of the lampshade. Trim to fit if necessary with a craft knife. Glue the top ring to the top of the lampshade. Glue the stamped medallions between each pair of curves, covering the cut ends. Fit to your lamp and enjoy the wonderful translucent glow!

Arabian Palace Clock

In the mountains of Lebanon, perched on a fragrant hillside and surrounded by cypresses and poplars, stands the beautiful Arabian palace of Beit Eddine. Built in the early nineteenth century by Italian architects for the ruler of Lebanon, it is a rich cornucopia of inlaid marble courtyards, dramatic stairways and sumptuous fountains. I had visited the palace as a child, and I returned recently to fill my sketchbook with dreamy images of another time. So here is a little clock that is inspired by an Arabian palace; hang it on your living room wall and it will give you a little touch of splendor!

Premo! Sculpey pearlescent clays are used to simulate the opulent marbles in this project, but you could use other brands as well.

materials>

> 2-ounce (60g) blocks of Premo! Sculpey polymer clay : 2 pearl, ⅛ block of gold, ⅟₁₆ block of ultramarine blue, small amounts of burnt umber and alizarin crimson
> several ceramic tiles to work on
> tracing paper and thin cardstock
> pasta machine or a roller and wood strips
> talcum powder
> cutters—I used the following shapes but you could substitute others
  ⅜" (10mm) triangle cutter
  ⅜" (10mm) star cutter
  ³⁄₁₆" (5mm) flower cutter
  ³⁄₁₆" (5mm) heart cutter
> a brush protector or circle cutter about ⅜" (10mm) diameter, or wide enough to cut a hole for the clock spindle to pass through.
> PVA glue
> quartz clock works and filigree-style hands
> craft knife

mixtures>

Marble the following:
> light blue marble = ½ block of pearl + ⅟₁₆ block ultramarine
> light gold marble = ¼ block of pearl + ⅛ block gold
> old rose marble = ¼ block of pearl + a pea size each of the alizarin crimson and burnt umber

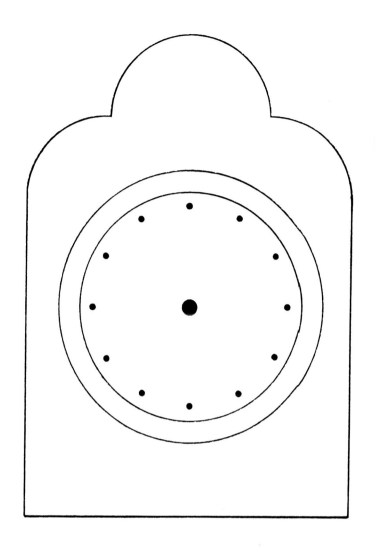

one | Preparation

Trace the clock front outline from the template onto thin cardstock and cut it out. Trace and cut out, separately, the two circles of the clock face to use later. Roll out a block of pearl clay until it is evenly shiny and ⅟₁₆" (1.5mm) thick. Lay this on a large tile and cut out the clock front.

Clock pattern must be enlarged at 118% to return to full size.

two | Cut decorative triangles

Roll out the marbled light gold clay on another tile at one setting thinner on your pasta machine. (If you are rolling by hand, roll the clay a little thinner with your roller.) Smear a dusting of talcum powder on the surface to prevent sticking, and use the triangle cutter to cut out lots of little triangles.

three | Add triangles

Use your knife to lift each triangle into place on the front of the clock, working round the arches, and laying the edge of each triangle along the edge of the clock. To turn the corner between two arches, cut a triangle in half and angle the two halves outward.

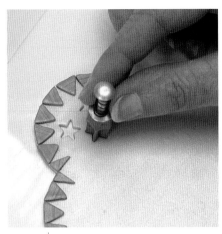

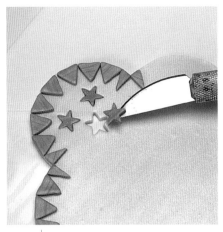

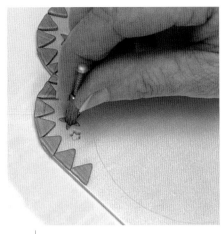

four | Cut out stars

To make the inlaid stars, brush the clock surface with talc and use the star cutter to cut out three stars in the center of the middle arch. Remove the clay using the point of a needle, taking care not to damage the clock front.

five | Inlay blue stars

Roll out the light blue marble clay to the same thickness as the light gold clay. Cut out stars in the same way as for the triangles and carefully insert them into the star spaces on the clock front.

six | Cut out flowers

The side arches each have an inlaid star flanked by two tiny flowers. Cut out and insert the inlaid stars in the same way as before, but use marbled light gold clay. Now use the tiny flower cutter to cut out the small flower shapes, one inside each star and one on either side.

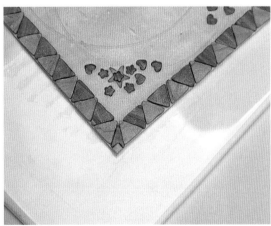

seven | Inlay again

Roll out the marbled old rose clay at the same thickness as the light gold clay. Cut and insert the tiny flower shapes as before. Use your knife tip to place the tiny pieces in position. Press over the inlays lightly with your fingertip to secure them in place.

eight | Finish clock face additions

Work around the rest of the clock front, using the photographs as a guide to the positioning of the inlays and applied triangles. The bottom part of the clock has light blue triangles alternating with light gold, and you will need to cut down the triangles to make neat corners. Use a combination of stars, hearts and flowers to decorate each bottom corner as before.

nine | Mark clock center

Lay the large circle template on the clock front and push a pin through the center of the card to mark the point where the clock works spindle should go. Use a brush protector or circle cutter to cut out a hole, centered on this exact spot and just wide enough for the spindle to pass through.

ten | Create pearl clay clock face

Roll out a sheet of pearl clay on a tile, at a thinner setting than the main clock front, and use the small circle template to cut out a circle for the clock face. Mark the center with a pin as before and cut out the hole for the spindle exactly in the center. Prick holes to mark the positions for the motifs that will be used instead of the clock numbers.

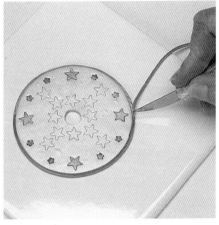

eleven | Decorate

Use the star cutter to inlay the top, bottom and side stars of the clock face with light gold clay. Use the flower cutter to inlay the light blue flowers that mark the remaining points of the clock face. Use the star cutter to impress stars onto the central area of the face in a regular pattern. Cut a ¹⁄₁₆" (1.5mm) thick strip of light gold from the gold sheet and wrap this around the outside of the face, butting and smoothing the join.

twelve | Finish and bake

Use the larger circle template to cut out the clock face backing in light blue clay, and make a hole in the center for the spindle as before. Bake all the pieces on their tiles for 30 to 40 minutes. Keep checking the pearl clay as it can brown if your oven gets too hot. Allow the pieces to cool and remove from the tiles.

thirteen | Attach face to the clock

Use PVA glue to glue the blue circle to the clock front, matching the spindle holes. Then glue the clock face on top of the blue circle, again matching the holes exactly.

fourteen | Assemble clock

Insert the hanger provided onto the clock works before you assemble the clock. Push the spindle of the clock works through the spindle hole in the clock. Screw on the spindle screw until the clock works are held firmly on the back of the clock with the hanger at the top.

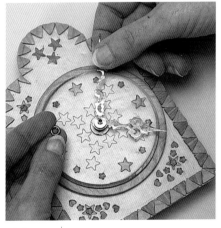

fifteen | Adjust hands

Push on the hour hand and then the minute hand. Adjust their positions to a whole hour. Finally screw down the smaller spindle screw to hold the hands in place.

Hang

The clock can now be hung on the wall by the metal hanger at the back of the clock works. Clock works can vary in design, so if yours is slightly different, follow the instructions provided.

))) WHEN I WAS A CHILD, *my elderly uncle and aunt lived in an old abbey with dark paneled rooms and winding staircases. My uncle had a splendid book-lined study complete with an enormous Victorian desk, leather-topped and creaking.*

the study

On the desk was a glorious collection of writing paraphernalia: marbled notebooks, exotic bookmarks and several beautiful fountain pens and inkpots.

SO HERE IS A COLLECTION *of polymer clay items that was inspired by my uncle Edward's study. The notebooks are simple to make but very sturdy, and the covers can be decorated in countless ways. A Celtic design is provided for the bookmarks, but you could photocopy your own drawings to create personalized versions. To complete the set, you can then make your own polymer clay pencils and pens.*

Polymer clay simulates tooled leather very successfully, and this project shows you how to create beautiful notebooks with polymer clay covers. A simple Japanese bookbinding method laces the pages so that the books are sturdy and stand up to regular use.

The notebooks can be made any size you like. I have used ordinary letter-size paper and cut it into fourths, but you could use an eighth of a sheet or even a sixteenth of a sheet for a tiny book. Try using handmade paper for the pages, or fill your book with favorite quotations and poems for a special gift.

materials>

) 2-ounce (60g) blocks of polymer clay: blue or color of your choice
) white letter-size paper—10 sheets will make a 40-page book
) paper guillotine or heavy-duty craft knife and a straightedge to cut against
) large tapestry needle
) thin cardstock
) four ceramic tiles at least 6" (15cm) square
) pasta machine or roller and wood strips
) tissue blade or long straight knife blade
) ⅛" (3mm) wide brush protector or round cutter
) small charms and scrap clay, or small stamps
) superglue
) gold metallic powder
) sandpaper
) quilt batting or scrap of cotton fabric
) matte varnish
) two binder clips
) 1" (25mm) wide masking tape
) marbled paper for the inside covers (or any attractive paper)
) PVA glue
) dark blue acrylic paint and paintbrush
) thin cord for lacing the covers

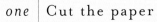

one | Cut the paper

Cut each sheet of paper into four pages. This is easy to do if you have a guillotine cutter, or you can use a knife and a straightedge to cut several sheets at a time.

two | Punch the lacing holes

Mark the position of the two lacing holes on one of the cut sheets, ⅜" (10mm) from the left-hand edge of the page and 1½" (4cm) from the top and bottom. Lay this sheet on top of several at a time, place the area to be punched over a block of clay and use the tapestry needle to punch a hole about 1/16" (1.5mm) wide. Repeat until all the pages have two holes in them.

three | Make the book cover template

Lay a punched page onto a sheet of stiff cardstock, aligning the left-hand edges. Draw a line ⅜" (10mm) away from the page edge on the other three sides so that the cover will be larger on these sides than the pages. Make small holes in the template at the position of the lacing holes.

four | Cut out the covers

Roll out the blue clay, about 1/16" (1.5mm) thick, on a tile. Lay the template on top and cut around it, removing the waste clay from around the cover. Mark the position of the lacing holes. Repeat for the back cover on another tile. There is no need to reverse the template because it is symmetrical. Do not move the covers from the tiles until after baking.

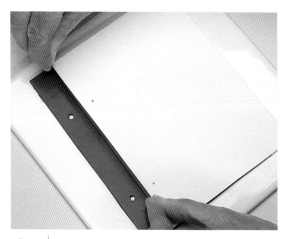

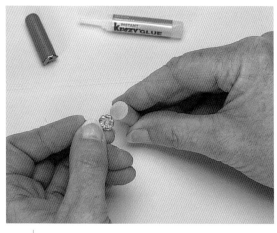

five | Cut spine pieces

Using the cover template as a guide, make a straight cut down the left side of the front cover, 5⁄16" (8mm) from the edge. Do not remove the clay—this strip will be separated from the front cover after baking and will form the front spine piece. Repeat for the back cover to make the back spine piece. Use the brush protector to cut neat lacing holes in the spine pieces of each cover.

six | Make the stamps

Form a log of scrap clay, about 3⁄8" (10mm) thick and 3" (7.5cm) long. Bake, and while it is still warm, cut in half to make two stamp handles. Glue a charm to the cut end of each with superglue.

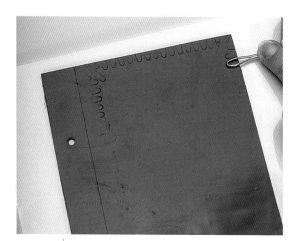

seven | Tool and decorate front cover

Use a ruler and needle to mark faint guidelines around the edges of the front cover, about 3⁄16" (5mm) from the edge. Mark a line of impressions all along the guidelines with the eye of a tapestry needle to suggest crimped leather. Remember to keep the line of impressions 1⁄4" (6mm) in from the spine edge because masking tape will cover this edge.

eight | Ready the stamp

Use your finger to apply gold powder to the surface of one of the stamps. You will need to reapply powder for each impression. The powder prevents the stamp from sticking to the clay and at the same time leaves a gilded impression.

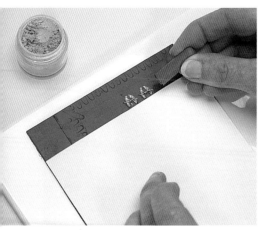  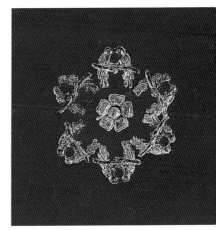

nine | **Stamp the cover top**

Try out the stamp on a piece of scrap clay so you know how hard to press for a clear impression. Lay a sheet of paper on the front cover as a guide and stamp all along the top of the cover.

ten | **Stamp the sides**

Use a different stamp to mark the corners of the cover. Stamp a line of impressions down each of the sides and the bottom edge.

eleven | **Stamp the center**

Make a decorative circle of impressions in the top center of the cover.

eleven | **Baking**

Lay a sheet of smooth paper over each cover and cover it with a second tile, laid face down, to keep it flat while baking. Bake the covers on the tiles for 50 minutes. When cool, remove the pieces from the tile, separating the spine pieces from the covers with your knife if necessary. If there are any blemishes on the surface, sand lightly and buff. The sanding will not damage the recessed gold impressions. Varnish the cover with matte varnish to protect the gold powder and give a smooth finish.

twelve | **Assemble the pages**

Stack the pages neatly and clamp them tightly together with the binder clips, ensuring that the lacing holes are aligned. Apply a strip of masking tape down the spine back, taking care not to cover the lacing holes.

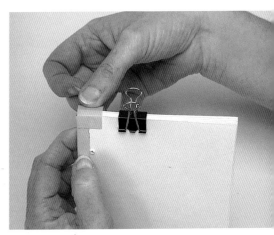

thirteen | **Apply tape**

Apply strips of tape to the top and bottom of the spine edge as well. This will help to keep the pages neatly contained inside the covers.

>*project two* Celtic Bookmarks

These bookmarks use motifs adapted from the Lindisfarne Gospels—extraordinary illuminated manuscripts that were created in Britain around 700 AD.

The bookmarks are made using a transfer technique that is a simple way of applying images to sheets of polymer clay. You must be sure to use a photocopier or laser printer that uses toner rather than ink or the technique will not work. Test with a small piece first to be sure that your prints will transfer successfully.

materials>

> 2-ounce (60g) blocks of polymer clay: 1 beige (Premo! Ecru)
> pasta machine or roller and wood strips
> tissue blade or long, straight knife blade
> fresh photocopy or laser print of the template provided
> scissors
> coloring pencils: red, blue, yellow, green, orange
> large tapestry needle
> ⅛" (3mm) wide brush protector or round cutter
> yellow embroidery silk
> small piece of stiff cardstock — business card size is ideal
> 12" (30cm) thin blue silk cord

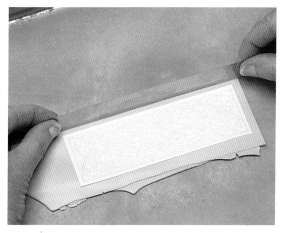

one | Prepare the photocopy

Trim the photocopy close to the outline all around. Color the image with the coloring pencils, pressing firmly so that the color is strongly applied.

two | Make the bookmark

Roll out some beige clay, about 1/16" (1.5mm) thick, and lay it onto a baking sheet lined with baking parchment. Place the image face down onto the clay, and use your blade to trim the bottom and sides of the bookmark, leaving a border of about 1/8" (3mm) down each side and 1/4" (6mm) at the bottom. Remove the waste clay from around the bookmark, and do not move the bookmark until after baking.

Bookmark pattern is full-size.

three | Trim the corners

Trim the top corners of the bookmark at an angle, leaving about 1/2" (13mm) of straight top edge in the center. If you find this hard to do by eyeballing it, cut out the shape in paper first to use as a guide to cut around.

four | Decorate the bottom

Mark along the bottom of the bookmark with the eye of a large tapestry needle to suggest tooled leather.

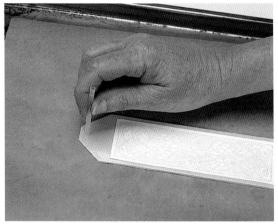

five | Cut the tassel hole

Use the brush protector to cut a neat hole in the top of the bookmark for the cord and tassel.

six | Press on image and bake

Burnish all over the back of the image with the pad of your finger. Work from the center outward so that you squeeze out any air bubbles. The pressure should be firm, but do not squash the clay. Bake for 20 minutes with the photocopy still in place.

seven | Remove image

When the clay is cool enough to handle, peel back the paper. The black lines of the photocopy and the coloring pencil will have transferred permanently onto the clay surface.

eight | Make the tassel

Make a small tassel by winding yellow embroidery silk around a business card and cutting to form a hank for the tassel skirt in the same way as for the large tassels on page 28, step 20. Attach the cord to the skirt in the same way (step 23), but first double the cord and bind the free ends together into the skirt so that the tassel hangs from a loop. Bind around the tassel with yellow silk, about ¼" (6mm) below where the cord emerges.

nine | Attach the tassel

Push the doubled end of the cord through the hole in the top of the bookmark and pull the tassel through the loop to secure.

Variation

The blue bookmark is made with blue pearl clay and the photocopy colored with white and purple coloring pencils.

Pearly Polyclay Pens

Polymer clay-covered pens have been popular with polymer clayers for years, but this is a new, improved version! The entire barrel of the pen is made with polymer clay so there is no need to worry whether a plastic pen barrel will survive baking. The ballpoint insert can be replaced when the pen runs out.

materials>

> 2-ounce (60g) block of polymer clay: 1 black

> ballpoint pen insert

> double-ended knitting needle, about ⅛" (3mm) thick

> tools of different thickness for grooving: paintbrush handle, kebab skewer, piece of thick card, etc.

> gold and silver pearlescent powders

> gloss varnish

> superglue

> tissue blade

> paintbrush

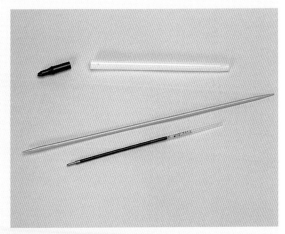

What you will need

Use the insert of an ordinary ballpoint pen. Inexpensive plastic pens are a good source of these—the inserts have a simple metal ballpoint tip attached to a tube of flexible plastic containing the ink. You can usually remove the insert by pulling off the end of the pen. Choose a knitting needle that is a little wider than the pen insert.

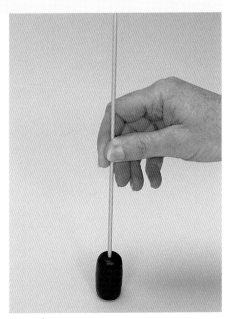

one | **Create short cylinder**

Form a 1½" (4cm) ball of black clay and roll it on your work surface to make a short cylinder. Stand this on end and pierce down through the center with the knitting needle. Push the knitting needle right through the clay so that the cylinder is in the center of the needle.

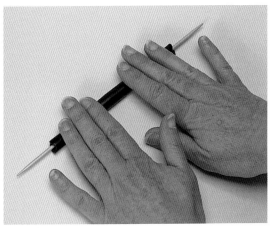

two | **Roll out clay cylinder**

Lay the knitting needle down on your work surface and roll it back and forth with your fingers as though you were forming a log. The clay will thin and lengthen along the knitting needle. Keep rolling until it is about ⅜" (10mm) thick, or until it is the thickness you would like your pen to be.

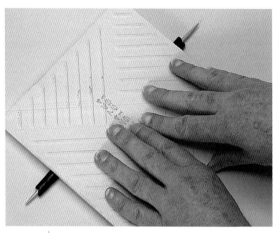

three | Smooth pen body

To make sure that the pen body sides are really straight and smooth, roll the clay back and forth a few times with the flat surface of a tile. If you find that the clay is pulling away from the needle, squeeze the clay all along its length and then continue rolling. The pen body should be able to turn slightly on the needle, but the hole around the needle should not be too large.

four | Trim end

With the pen body still on the needle (it is not removed until after baking), trim one end with your blade by pressing it onto the clay while you rotate the pen. You will find you can cut neatly right around the body in this way.

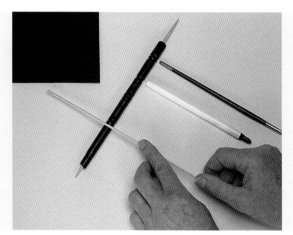

five | Groove pen body

Starting at the trimmed end, "groove" the clay: Hold a kebab skewer onto the clay surface at right angles to the pen and press down as you push the handle back and forth. This will rotate the clay body and the pressure will make an even groove all around. The tools used to groove the clay in the photograph are placed next to the various grooves they have made: a kebab skewer, the old pen body, and a paintbrush handle. You can make single grooves or groups to vary the design.

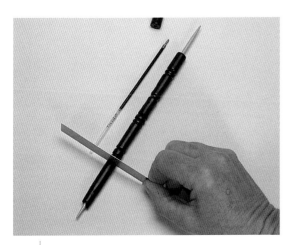

six | Determine pen length

Lay the pen insert alongside your grooved pen body so you can see how long the pen needs to be. Cut the pen body so that it is about ¼" (6mm) shorter than the insert. The ballpoint tip of the insert will need to protrude out of the pen body after assembly.

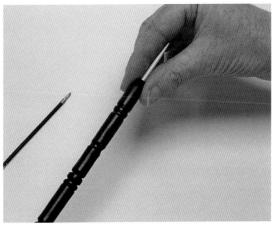

seven | Pinch ballpoint end

Pinch the ballpoint end of the pen into a gently curved point around the knitting needle. Check the length and trim the other end again if necessary.

eight | Make the pen end

Form a ⅜" (10mm) ball of black clay and press it down onto a tile with the flat pad of your finger to make a disk about ½" (13mm) across. Form a ⁵⁄₁₆" (8mm) ball and press this onto the disk, flattening it slightly. Finally press a ¼" (6mm) ball onto the top. Leave on the tile for baking.

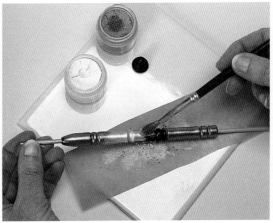

nine | Apply the powder

Hold the pen by the knitting needle and brush it all over with bands of gold and silver powders. Brush the pen end in the same way. The underlying black clay will make the powders look really rich.

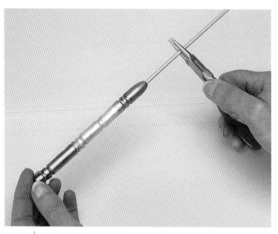

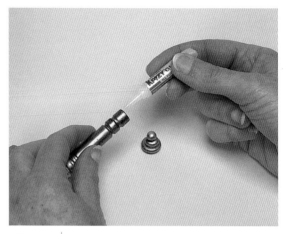

ten | Bake and remove needle

Bake the pen and pen end for 30 minutes. When the pen is still warm but cool enough to handle, gently ease the knitting needle out of the clay. You may find it easier to grip the knitting needle with pliers as you do this.

eleven | Attach decorative end and varnish

Attach the decorative end with superglue. Varnish the pen and pen end to protect the powder. Push the insert into the pen body to check that it is the right length. You can trim the end of the pen body, or cut off the end of the insert if one is too long. Glue the pen end to the pen body.

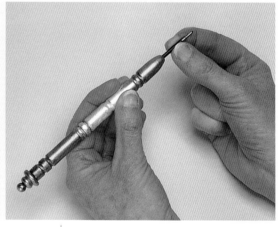

twelve | Insert ballpoint pen

Push the ballpoint pen insert into the pen body as far as it will go. The tip should protrude about ¼" (6mm) from the end. The insert should stay in by itself, but if it is loose, use a little tacky glue around the tip to hold it in place. When the pen runs out, you can replace the insert by pulling it out with pliers and inserting a new one.

Polyclay Pencils >*project four*

Polymer clay pencils are great fun to make and they can be sharpened like ordinary wooden pencils. Use a really strong clay for this project, and do not make the pencils too thin or they will bend easily and snap the lead inside them.

The leads used in this project are draftsmen's clutch pencil leads and can be obtained from art supply stores. Marbled clay is used here but you can decorate your pencils in many other ways such as with simple cane slices or pearlescent powders.

materials>

⟩ polymer clay: small quantities of clay in two or more colors for marbling. You will need the equivalent of about half a 2-ounce (60g) block of clay per pencil.

⟩ 2mm-thick clutch pencil lead

⟩ craft knife

⟩ pencil sharpener for wide pencils

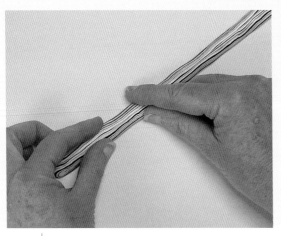

one | Create marbled logs

Marble the different colored clays together, keeping the streaks parallel, until all the streaks are thin but still distinct (see page 18). Form into a log about ½" (13mm) diameter and 8" (20cm) long. Press this down on your work surface to give it a semicircular cross section all along its length.

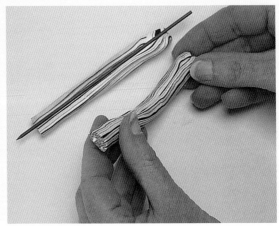

two | Add pencil lead

Cut the log in half and turn one half so that the flat side is uppermost. Lay the pencil lead centrally along this, and then cover it with the other half, flat side down, to sandwich the lead in the middle of the log. Note that one end of the lead is pointed. This will be the end to sharpen.

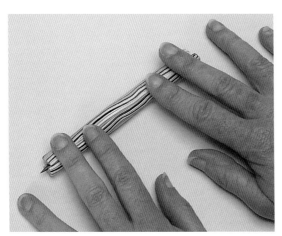

three | Reform logs

Press the two logs together to make a single log, but be careful not to break the lead inside the clay. Now roll the log on your work surface to consolidate the two halves, and thin the log to about ⅜" (10mm) thick.

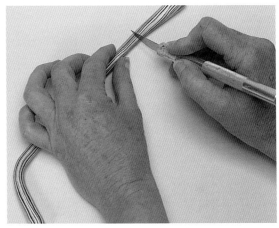

four | Trim excess clay

As you roll the log thinner, it will extend at each end beyond the pencil lead. If you bend the clay at the ends, you will be able to see where the lead is. Trim off the excess clay at intervals as you roll to stop the log from becoming too unmanageable. You can use a tile to smooth the log as for the pens on page 52.

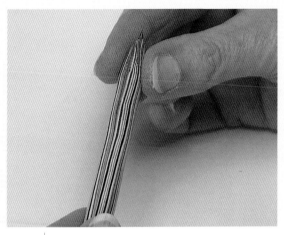

five | Pinch writing end

When the pencil is the right thickness all along its length, trim the end covering the pointed lead until you can see the lead. Pinch this end into a point.

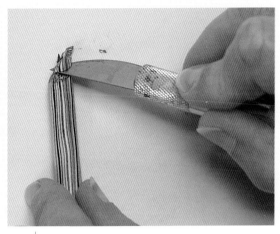

six | Sharpen writing end

Use your knife to "sharpen" the soft clay at the pointed end of the lead. After baking, this will make the first sharpening easier.

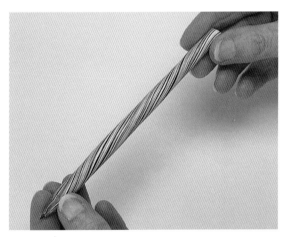

seven | Twist to form spiral

Trim the unsharpened end of the pencil about ½" (13mm) beyond the end of the lead (locate it within the clay as before, by bending the clay). Make sure that the clay at this end is sealed, or the lead will be pushed out of the clay when you write. Gently twist the clay around the pencil so that the marbled lines form a spiral pattern.

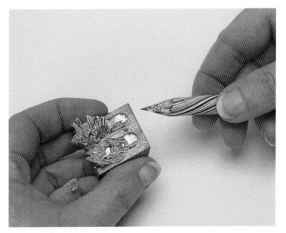

eight | Bake and sharpen

Bake the pencil for 30 minutes to be sure that the clay is really strong. While the clay is still warm, sharpen the pencil into a neat point with the pencil sharpener.

the *the* dining room

))) **OUR DINING ROOM IS** *attached to the kitchen, so on ordinary days it doubles as a craft room, a snack room, a parcel packing room, a cup-of-tea room when the neighbors call and many other types of room, too. But on high days and holidays, it becomes a Very Special Occasion Room, and that is when I like to fill it with beautiful things to help with the transformation.*

THIS CHAPTER SHOWS YOU *how to make fragile-looking candleholders in misty colors to transport your dinner guests; a special occasion cruet set that would not look out of place at a banquet; and a trivet that has origins in a Roman villa. Finally, you can make a unique set of cutlery that can be adapted to match the color of your dining room.*

>*project one* Silver Shells Cruet Set

Here is a cruet set with a difference! A cockleshell is used to make a Victorian-style salt cellar, complete with a little shell spoon. It is paired with a matching upright pepper pot. The Victorians favored small open pots, or cellars, for their salt and often had individual cellars at each place setting. They kept pepper in a shaker pot, though, no doubt to prevent sneezing!

materials>

) 2-ounce (60g) blocks of polymer clay: 1 black and scrap clay for making the molds

) collection of small seashells, ¾" (2cm) to 1" (2.5cm) long

) cockleshell or similar shaped shell for salt cellar, about 2" (5cm) across

) 1½" (3cm) circle cutter

) talcum powder

) glass pepper pot with silver colored top

) PVA glue

) silver metallic powder

) soft paintbrush

) 18-gauge silver plated wire

) fine-nosed pliers

) ½" (13mm) cockleshell or similar, for salt spoon

) superglue

) gloss varnish

) roller

) craft knife

) tile (optional)

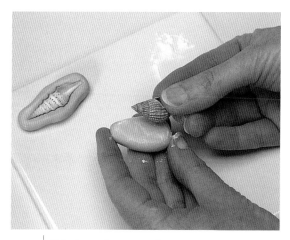

one | Make clay ovals

Knead a ball of scrap clay until it is really soft. You will need a
piece of clay a bit larger than the shell you are going to mold.
Shape the clay into an oval and flatten it so that its surface is
larger all around than your shell. Brush the surface with
talcum powder.

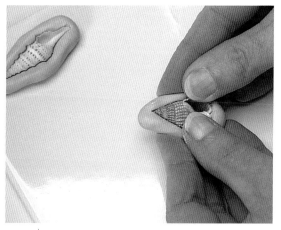

two | Press shell into clay

Choose the side of the shell that will make the best impression
and press this firmly into the clay. Pull the edges of the clay up
all around the shell until they reach halfway up the sides. Keep
up a firm, even pressure to avoid making a double image.

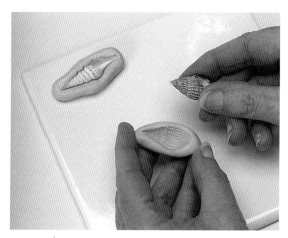

three | Remove shell and bake

Gently ease the shell out of the clay and you will be left with a
detailed impression in the clay. Take impressions of several different shells. Bake all the molds for 30 minutes.

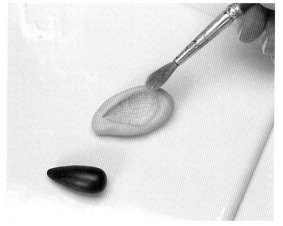

four | Mold the clay shells

Shape a piece of black clay into a pointed oval about the same
size and shape as the cavity in the mold. Brush the inside of
the mold with talcum powder and tap out the excess.

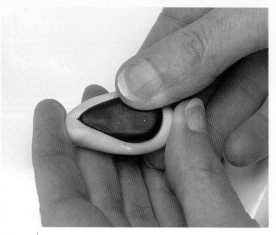

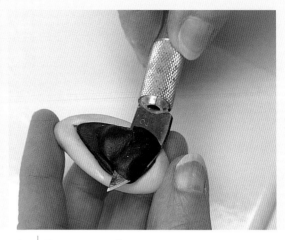

five | Push clay into mold

Place the point of the clay oval into the point of the mold and push the clay firmly into the mold.

six | Remove clay

Flatten the surface of the clay with your finger and trim off any excess with your knife. Let the clay protrude a little above the surface of the mold so that it is easier to remove. Carefully pry the clay out of the mold with your knife.

seven | Trim excess clay

Place the molded shell, flat side down, on your work surface and trim away any excess around the edges. The molded shell is now ready to use. Make about six molded shells for the salt cellar and eight for the pepper pot.

eight | Make the salt cellar

Roll out a sheet of clay, 1/16" (1.5mm) thick, on a tile. Cut out a circle of clay about 1½" (4cm) diameter.

nine | Add molded shells

Press a ring of molded shells around the outside of the circle of clay. Be careful not to squash the shells as you press them on—apply pressure with a tool in a place that is not visible. Press the cockleshell onto the clay shells, rearranging them if necessary so that it rests level.

ten | Brush on silver powder

Brush silver powder over all the visible parts of the molded shells with a soft paintbrush. The powder will highlight all the beautiful textures on the shells. Leave the piece on the tile to bake with the pepper pot.

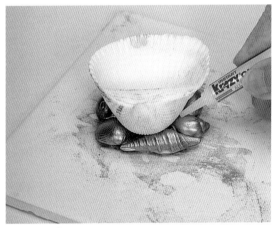

eleven | Make the pepper pot

Brush the base of the pepper pot with a thin coat of PVA glue. This will help the molded clay shells to adhere to the glass. Press on the molded shells, overlapping them slightly and arranging them to fit together pleasingly. Brush with silver powder and bake with the salt cellar on the tile for 30 minutes. Allow to cool.

twelve | Add superglue

Without moving the cockleshell, squeeze a little superglue underneath it, where it rests on the molded shells. This will bond it more tightly to its supporting shells. (Do not move it first, or you will never be able to find the exact spot it fitted into again!) Varnish all the silver shells to protect the powder.

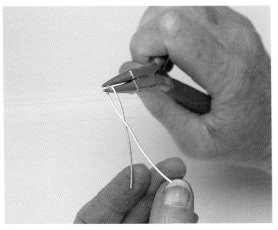

thirteen | Make the salt spoon

To make the spoon handle, first fold the length of wire in half. Grip the folded end with the pliers and, holding the free ends in your hand, twist the wire to make a twined handle. If the wire is very stiff, use a second pair of pliers.

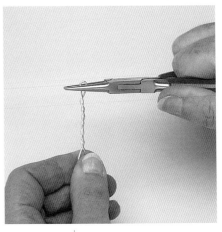

fourteen | Adjust wire

Try to keep the twists as even as possible all along the double length of wire. Leave the free ends of the wire untwisted for the last ½" (13mm).

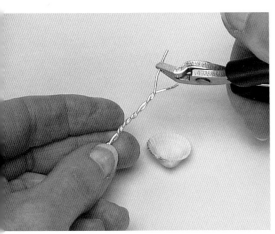

fifteen | Add cradle

Shape the two untwisted ends of the wire into a prong shape, bending them into a gentle curve that will cradle the small shell. The wires need to touch all along the bottom of the shell to make a good bond when glued. Trim the wires so that they do not stick out beyond the shell.

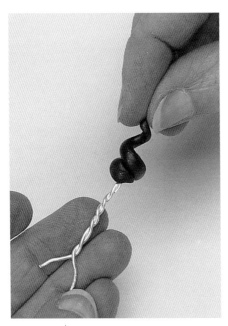

sixteen | Add clay end

To make a decorative end to the spoon handle, form a ⅜" (10mm) ball of black clay and shape it into a 1½" (4cm) long log. Point one end of the log and twirl it into a spiral around the wire at the top of the spoon handle, pressing it onto the wire to secure. Brush with silver powder and bake on the wire for 20 minutes.

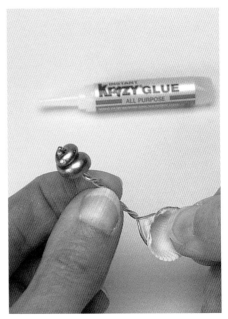

seventeen | Assemble

Varnish the silver spiral to protect the powder. Glue the small shell onto the wire prongs using superglue. Fill the cockleshell with salt and the pepper pot with pepper, and place on your party table!

Pearl Veneer Cutlery *>project two*

Fabulous whorls of almost holographic patterns decorate this unusual cutlery. The sumptuous effects are created using millefiori caning techniques with pearlescent Premo! Sculpey. This remarkable technique was first developed by Pier Voulkos, Mike Buesseler and others in the United States.

When this type of pearlescent clay is repeatedly rolled out into a sheet, the saucer-shaped mica particles in the clay are all forced to lie horizontally. The flat surface of the clay then appears shiny while the cut edges at the sides look dull. In this project, alternating sheets of dull and shiny clay are rolled into a spiral cane and used to make the veneer for the cutlery handles.

You will need to use pearlescent clay that contains mica particles such as Premo! Sculpey. The effects do not work with other pearl or metallic polymer clays. The cutlery is hand washable.

materials>

〉 2-ounce (60g) blocks of Premo! Sculpey polymer clay: 2 pearl and 1 blue pearl

〉 stainless steel cutlery in a simple design

〉 pasta machine or roller and wood strips

〉 sharp blade

〉 sand paper and quilt batting

〉 tile (optional)

mixtures>

〉 Light blue pearl = 2 parts pearl + 1 part blue pearl

one | Roll out clay sheet

Roll out a sheet of light blue pearl clay, fold in half and roll again. Repeat several times until the surface of the clay is uniformly shiny. Finally, roll out the sheet about ⅛" (3mm) thick and lay it on a tile. Trim the edges to make a rectangle 4" x 6" (10cm x 15cm)

two | Cut sheets and stack

Cut the rectangle in half and place one half on top of the other. Cut in half again, and again stack the two halves one on top of the other. Repeat once more to make a stacked block approximately 1½" (4cm) wide, 2" (5cm) long and 1" (2.5cm) tall.

three | Trim edges of block

Trim the edges of the block. You will find that while the top surface of the block is shiny, when you take a slice from any of the sides, it has a dull appearance.

four | Stack shiny and dull sheets

Roll out another shiny sheet of light blue pearl, as thin as you can—about ½₂" (1mm) thick—and cut a rectangle 2" (5cm) wide and 5" (13cm) long. Lay this on the tile. Now cut slices from the dull long side of your block, about ½₂" (1mm) thick. Lay these side by side on top of the shiny rectangular sheet. Butt the edges of the slices together so that there are no gaps.

five | Press joins and trim

When the rectangle is covered with dull sheets, press the joins together lightly to consolidate them and trim the double sheet if necessary. Now press along the edge of one of the short ends to flatten it.

six | Roll up clay

Ease the flattened edge off the tile and, beginning at this end, roll up the two sheets together tightly like a jellyroll. As you roll, press gently to expel any air bubbles that might be caught inside the roll.

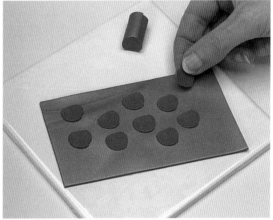

seven | Slice cane

When the two sheets are tightly rolled up together, press lightly to consolidate the roll. You now have a cane for slicing, but do not try to reduce it or the effects will be lost. Cut a slice off one end to trim it and then cut lots of ¹⁄₁₆" (1.5mm) thick slices. Keep your blade as vertical as possible and try to cut the slices evenly and of the same thickness. The spiral effect of rolling the two sheets together is already very clear.

eight | Create the veneer

Roll out a sheet of shiny clay at the thickest setting on your pasta machine, about ⅛" (3mm) thick. Lay on the slices of spiral cane in a regular pattern.

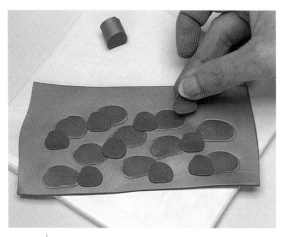

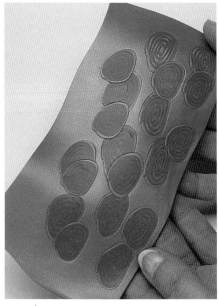

nine | Apply more slices

Pass the sheet with the applied slices through your pasta machine on the same thickest setting (or roll over the sheet lightly with your roller). Now apply another layer of slices, slightly overlapping the first slices.

ten | Thin the sheet

Pass the sheet through the pasta machine again in the same direction as before and still on the same setting. Now set the pasta machine to roll at about 1⁄16" (1.5mm) thick, a medium setting, and pass the sheet through again. This will smooth the surface and accentuate the effect.

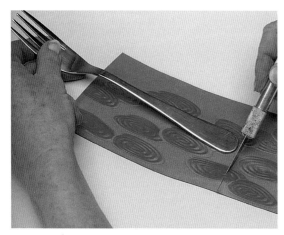

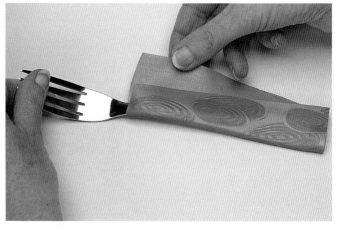

eleven | Cut clay for handle

Finally pass the sheet through one last time on one setting thinner. The spiral lozenges will elongate and look like flying saucers on a background of light blue. Lay the handle of the fork on the sheet and cut out enough clay to cover the handle.

twelve | Cover the fork handle

Turn the clay sheet over and lay the fork handle on the back. Fold the sheet over the top of the fork handle, moving it if necessary to position the patterning to best advantage.

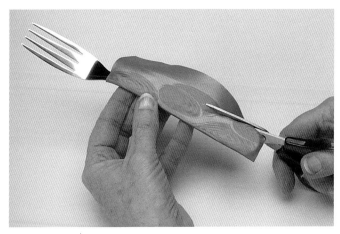

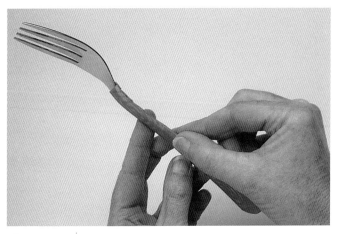

thrirteen | Trim clay

Use a pair of scissors to trim the clay all along the fork handle, close to the edge, which you can feel through the clay.

fourteen | Join and smooth clay

Press the two edges of the sheet together along the side and end of the fork handle, smoothing the join by stroking it with your fingers.

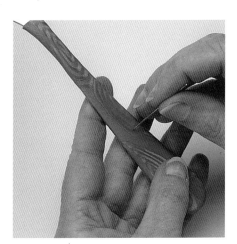

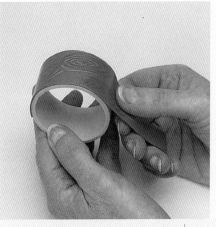

fifteen | Remove bubbles

Use a pin to pierce any bubbles that appear under the clay and press them to expel the air. If you do not do this, they will accentuate during baking as the air inside expands.

sixteen | Trim and bake

Finally, trim the top edge of the handle neatly. Repeat to cover the knife and spoon handles to make a matching set. Bake all the pieces on baking parchment for 30 minutes. When cool, sand and buff to bring out the gleaming design.

Make the napkin ring |

Follow the instructions on page 81 for making the sides of a round box using pearl clay. This baked cylinder forms the base for the napkin ring. Now cover the pearl ring with a sheet of spiral-covered light blue pearl to match the cutlery. Bake again, and then sand and buff as for the cutlery handles.

These candleholders were inspired by the work of Gallé, the famous French glass designer, They simulate the dreamy frosted glass and cameo effects that were his specialty in the late nineteenth century. Transparent Liquid Sculpey, painted on the glass, provides the frosted look, while appliqué images in tinted translucent clay give the effect of cameo.

A conical-shaped drinking glass works best for this project, but you could use a tumbler instead. You will need to adjust the template to fit the shape of your glass.

Use the instructions to make a matching pair of candleholders for an elegant dining table centerpiece.

materials>

> 2-ounce (60g) blocks of polymer clay: 1 translucent and small amounts of blue-green and black
> Transparent Liquid Sculpey
> paintbrush
> denatured alcohol (methylated spirits)
> small mixing palette
> Viridian oil paint
> tapestry needle, plus a darning needle or pointed tool
> conical-shaped drinking glass
> tracing paper and pencil
> pasta machine or roller
> night-light or votive candle
> craft knife
> tile (optional)

mixtures>

> dark sea green = ½" (13mm) ball of black + ½" (13mm) ball of blue-green
> light translucent green = ⅛ block translucent + ¼" (6mm) ball of dark sea green
> dark translucent green = ¼ block translucent + ⅝" (15mm) ball of dark sea green
> midtranslucent green = ⅜" (10mm) ball of light translucent green + ⅜" (10mm) ball of dark translucent green

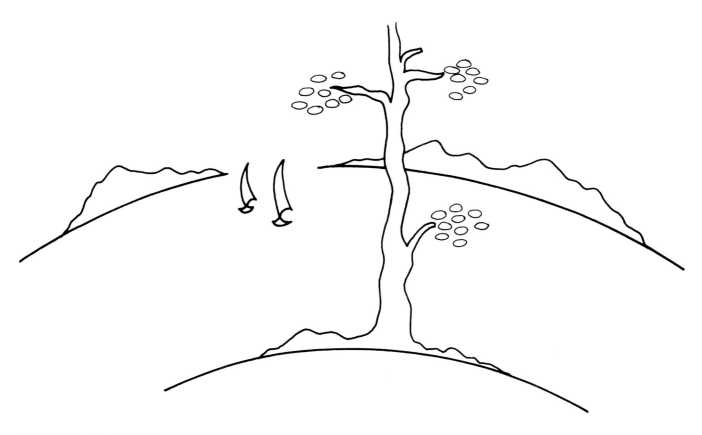

Candleholder pattern is full-size.

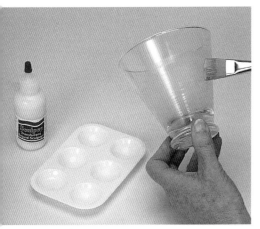

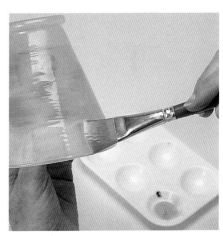

one | Frost the glass

Wipe over the glass with alcohol to ensure that it is really clean and allow it to dry. Paint the outside of the glass with a thin coat of the Liquid Sculpey, leaving the top 1" (2.5cm) unpainted. Use horizontal strokes and brush out any thicker areas or they may run during baking and form drips.

two | Create pastel green

Squeeze a spot of Viridian oil paint onto the side of the palette. Use a thick needle or a cocktail stick to stir a dab into the Liquid Sculpey to make a pale pastel green. Keep stirring until all streakiness has disappeared.

three | Paint and bake

Paint the top 1" (2.5cm) of the glass with the pastel green, blending the join. It is easier to do this if you hold the glass upside-down with your hand inside to steady it. Stand the glass upright on a parchment-lined baking sheet and bake for 20 minutes to set the Liquid Sculpey. Cool the glass slowly in the oven with the door open to avoid shattering the glass.

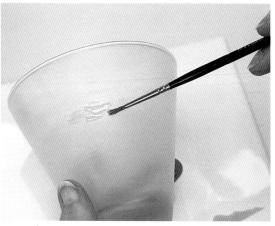

four | Make the far island

Trace the far island template onto tracing paper and check that the curve of the horizon is horizontal when applied to your glass, adjusting it if necessary. Roll out a sheet of the light translucent green mixture as thinly as possible, and place the tracing on it. Scribe along the lines with the point of a darning needle to mark the shape onto the clay and then cut it out with your knife. Remove the excess clay.

five | Brush on Liquid Sculpey

Brush a thin coat of Liquid Sculpey onto a horizontal strip about one-third of the way down the glass where you will place the island. This provides a key to help the island stick to the baked Liquid Sculpey.

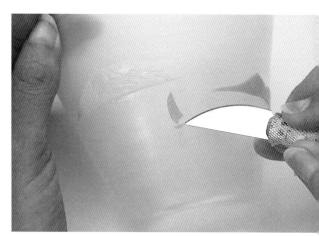

six | Add cutout island

Press the cutout island onto the glass and smooth the cut edges to chamfer them down to the glass surface.

seven | Texture

Use the blunt point of the tapestry needle to scribe lines down the mountain sides for texture. When the candle is lit inside the glass, these will show as lighter streaks.

eight | Make the near island and boat

Cut out and apply the near island and the smaller boat in mid-transparent green clay in the same way. Position the near island a little lower down the glass than the far island.

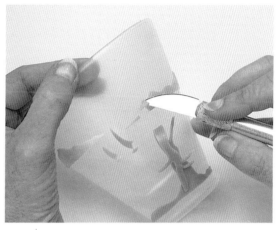

nine | Make the large boat and foreground tree

Cut out and apply the large boat in dark translucent green. Cut out the large foreground tree in dark translucent green. Lift this into place on the glass, with the trunk lying over the end of the near island. Cut through the island on either side of the trunk.

ten | Trim excess clay

Fold back the upper part of the tree and lift out the section of island behind it. Press the tree back into place in the gap using a thin smear of Liquid Sculpey to help it adhere as before. This is to avoid a double layer of clay where the tree crosses the island.

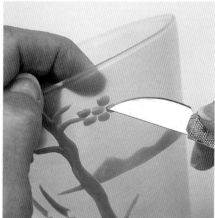

eleven | Form clay log

Brush a thin coat of Liquid Sculpey onto the area around the ends of the small branches. Form a ³⁄₁₆" (5mm) thick log of dark green translucent clay and cut off the end to straighten it. Cut a ¹⁄₁₆" (1.5mm) thick slice with your knife, lifting the slice onto the blade as you cut.

twelve | Add foliage

Transfer the slice from your blade onto the glass by turning your blade over to press the slice down. Repeat to make a series of leafy shapes all around the small branches of the foreground tree.

thirteen | Create texture and reflection

Scribe along the lines of the trunk with the tapestry needle as before to suggest bark and highlights on the trunk. Use a fine brush to paint streaks of the green-tinted Liquid Sculpey under the boats and islands to suggest reflections. Bake the glass for 30 minutes and allow it to cool slowly in the oven as before. Place a votive candle in the glass.

Roman Mosaic Trivet

Polymer clay is a perfect material for making mosaics. The little tiles, or "tesserae," can be cut straight from unkneaded blocks of clay to whatever size you choose. These are then baked and glued into a pattern on a flat or curved surface. In this project, Transparent Liquid Sculpey is used to grout the mosaic for a very strong result.

The mosaic floor of a 1600-year-old Roman villa inspired the design for this project. The trivet can be used as a pleasing centerpiece for a dining table and will protect your table surface from hot serving dishes. It will withstand temperatures up to 300°F (150°C), but do not use it for pans taken straight from the stovetop.

materials>

⟩ 2-ounce (60g) blocks of polymer clay: 1 white; 1⁄2
  each of black, ochre, copper, leaf green and beige (Premo! Ecru)

⟩ tissue blade

⟩ ruler, soft pencil and tracing paper

⟩ denatured alcohol (methylated spirits)

⟩ PVA glue

⟩ 8" (20cm) square plain white ceramic tile

⟩ Transparent Liquid Sculpey

⟩ glue spreader or piece of thick cardstock

⟩ rag

⟩ 8" (20cm) square of dark green felt

⟩ craft knife

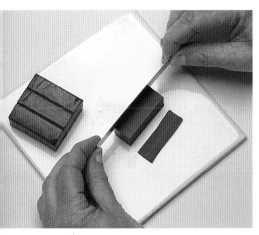

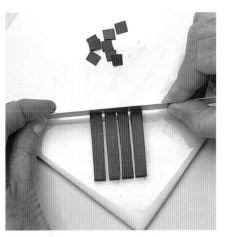

one | Cut up the clay block

Cut a rectangular bar of clay straight from an unkneaded block, and trim the long sides to give a cross section of ½" (13mm) square.

two | Divide again

Cut the bar in half lengthwise and then in half again to give four bars, each about ¼" (6mm) square in cross-section. They will probably end up slightly rectangular rather than completely square, and this is fine—Roman tesserae were slightly rectangular!

three | Create tesserae

Arrange the four bars in a row and use your blade to cut across all four at a time. This is a quick way of making lots of tesserae. Try to cut as evenly as possible—each slice should be about ¹⁄₁₆" (1.5mm) thick. Look down onto the bars as you cut and keep your blade as straight as possible. Do not worry if there is some variation—this is conveniently Roman as well!

four | Bake

Pile the tesserae into heaps on a baking sheet covered with baking parchment. Keep the colors separate, but there is no need to spread the pieces out. Bake for 20 to 30 minutes and allow the tesserae to cool. Some may have stuck together a little, but they are easily pulled apart.

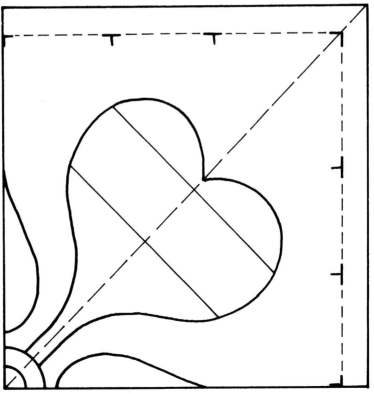

Trivet pattern is full-size.

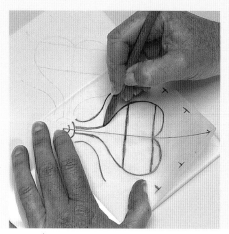

five | Transfer the design

Wipe over the tile with alcohol to de-grease the surface. Using a soft pencil and a ruler, draw lines joining the opposite corners of the tile to locate the center. Trace the template onto tracing paper with the soft pencil. Flip the tracing over and position it on a quarter of the tile, matching the center points. Draw over the backs of the lines to transfer the design, then repeat for the other quarters. The pencil marks will be faint but visible.

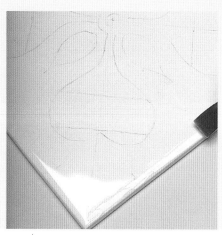

six | Apply coat of glue

Apply a thin coat of PVA glue along one edge of the tile. You should only apply glue to a small area at a time so that you have time to press on the tesserae before the glue dries.

seven | Apply black tesserae

First apply a line of black tesserae around the edge of the tile. Leave slight spaces between them, which are later filled with grout. Outline the heart shapes with black tesserae, working just inside the pencil line and keeping the edges of the tesserae aligned around the curves.

eight | Fill gaps

Fill the V-shaped gaps around the outside of the curves with black tesserae cut to shape. The baked clay cuts easily with a craft knife. Fill any other spaces in the outline with small pieces cut to the required shapes.

nine | Fill in hearts

Fill the inside of each heart outline with beige, ochre and copper tesserae following the pencil lines. First glue a line of beige tesserae along the pencil line dividing the beige from the ochre sections. This will keep you straight as you fill in the remaining lines of colors. Cut the tesserae to fit at the edges where they meet the black outline pieces.

ten | Create border

To make the stepped border, first glue a copper tessera at each point marked on the template against the black border. Then glue a tessera on either side of the first and one above it. Fill in with white tesserae between, cutting the pieces to fit. This way, you will be sure that the copper border groups are evenly spaced, regardless of how irregular in size your tesserae are!

eleven | Create leaves

Continue to fill in the white area, working from each side of the tile in parallel lines toward the center. Cut the white tesserae to fit wherever they meet a curved edge. Fill in the leaf shapes with leaf green tesserae, cutting them to shape around the tip and the base of each leaf. Fill in with white tesserae around the leaves.

twelve | Dry thoroughly

The center of the design consists of a large white square surrounded by a black ring made from alternating black squares and triangles. Do not worry if there is a bit of extra space around the central square—this will be filled with grout. When the mosaic is finished, leave the glue to dry thoroughly.

thirteen | Grout the mosaic

Squeeze lines of Liquid Sculpey along the spaces between the tesserae. When it is baked, the Liquid Sculpey will be translucent and have a matte finish so it will hardly show and will pull the design together beautifully.

fourteen | Remove excess

Use a glue spreader or piece of card to squeegee the Liquid Sculpey into the spaces between the tesserae. Scrape the excess off the surface of the tesserae and into the spaces between, adding more Liquid Sculpey as necessary. Finally wipe the surface of the mosaic with a soft rag to remove excess liquid.

fifteen | Bake and finish

Bake the mosaic for 30 to 40 minutes. Remove from the oven and allow to cool. Lay the mosaic on a piece of green felt and mark around it with a pen. Cut out the felt and use PVA glue to glue it firmly to the back of the tile. This will protect your tabletop from scratches.

 the bedroom

))) POLYMER CLAY IS TRULY *remark-*
able when it comes to simulating a wide range of
materials. Creating artifacts in precious metals
would normally entail a long apprenticeship; but
with polymer clays and pearlescent powders, you can make arti-
facts of simulated silver and bronze using only your modeling skills.

THE BEDROOM IS THE *place for family heir-*
looms, particularly silver photo frames and trinket boxes; and
the following projects show you how to make them yourself using
polymer clay! The Art Nouveau frame in simulated silver and
enamel is a perfect setting for the photo of a favorite person. The
trinket boxes, with their delicate trailed designs, are so useful for
all the pins, buttons and other bits and pieces that inevitably
accumulate on a dressing table. And the little pomander, which
is inspired by Elizabethan metalwork, will fragrance the clothes
in your closet with your favorite potpourri.

>*project one* Trinket Boxes

Pearly trinket boxes spangled with dainty stars and hearts make stylish artifacts for the dressing table. The box in this project is made from pearlescent clay using a card tube as a simple former. Translucent Liquid Sculpey, adapted to cold enamel techniques, decorates the lids.

Try using this technique to make boxes in a variety of sizes—foil-covered bottled and jars make perfect formers and you can vary the height of the boxes as well.

materials>

> 2-ounce (60g) blocks of polymer clay: 1 pearl

> pasta machine or roller and wood strips

> 12" (30cm) metal ruler, about 1¼" (3cm) wide

> paper towel insert, smoothly covered with foil and taped for a former

> tapestry needle

> darning needle

> ceramic tiles

> talcum powder

> sandpaper and quilt batting

> Fun-Tak or Blu-Tak (reusable putty adhesive)

> Transparent Liquid Sculpey

> paintbrush

> oil paint: white, blue, violet

> small palette for mixing

> superglue

> craft knife

one | Make the box sides

Roll out the pearl clay into a sheet, fold in half and roll out again several times until uniformly shiny. Roll the sheet to about ³⁄₃₂" (2mm) thick. Lay the ruler on the sheet and use it as a cutting edge to cut a strip of clay, 1¼" (3cm) wide and about 8" (20cm) long.

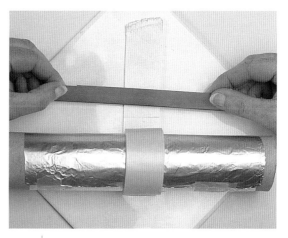

two | Roll around former

Roll the clay strip around the foil-covered former, keeping the edges of the strip as straight as possible. Keep rolling until the beginning of the strip meets the clay surface again and makes a faint impression. Unroll a little and trim the clay on this line.

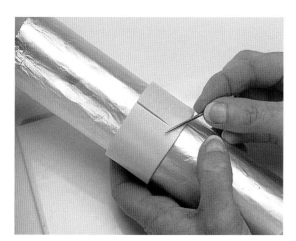

three | Join, smooth and bake

The strip should now be the right length for the two ends to meet in a butt joint. Smooth the join with the side of a tapestry needle. Bake the box sides on the former for 20 minutes. Allow to cool and slip the baked clay off the former.

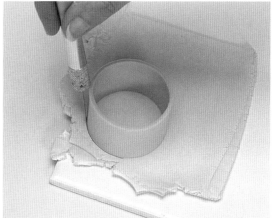

four | Make the box lid

Roll out another sheet of pearl clay, ¹⁄₁₆" (1.5mm) thick, and lay it on the tile. Smear the clay surface with talc to prevent sticking and place the baked box sides on it. Cut around the outside of the box for the lid, holding your knife blade as upright as possible for a neat edge. Remove the waste clay from around the lid and leave the lid on the tile.

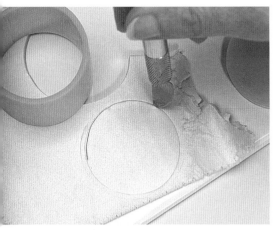

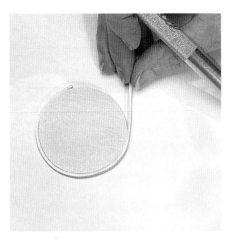

five | Make lid flange

Place the remaining sheet on a spare bit of the tile and press the box sides on again, firmly, to make an impression. Remove the box and cut around the inside of the resulting mark to make the inner lid. This will be glued to the underside of the lid after baking so that the lid fits snugly onto the box.

six | Make the box base

Roll another ³⁄₃₂" (2mm) thick sheet of clay and, using no talcum powder this time, press the bottom of the box sides firmly onto the sheet. Cut around the outside and remove the waste clay. Use your knife to smooth the join between the soft clay of the box base and the baked sides. Bake all the pieces on the tile for 30 minutes. When cool, sand and buff any rough areas.

seven | Refine the lid

Place the box lid on a tile, best side up. Cut an 8" (20 cm) long strip of clay, about ¹⁄₁₆" (1.5mm) wide, from a ¹⁄₁₆" (1.5mm) thick sheet. Wrap this around the outside of the lid, smoothing the joins. This will make the lid slightly larger in diameter than the box and will give a better finish.

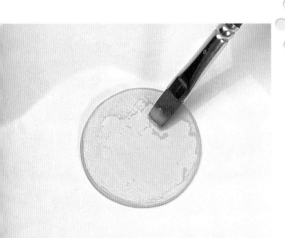

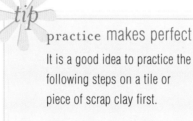

tip

practice makes perfect

It is a good idea to practice the following steps on a tile or piece of scrap clay first.

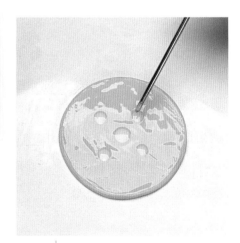

eight | Add Liquid Sculpey

Fix the lid to the tile with a tiny scrap of Fun-Tak underneath it to stop it from sliding around. Brush a thin coat of Liquid Sculpey over the surface of the lid. Mix a little white oil paint into about a teaspoonful of Liquid Sculpey on your palette.

nine | Create white pools

Dip the tapestry needle tip into the white Liquid Sculpey to collect a drop on the end. Touch the center of the lid with the drop and slowly lift the needle vertically upward from the surface. A thread of Liquid Sculpey will extend from the needle and this will part and drop back as you lift, so keep the needle above the pool of color. Repeat to make four more pools around the central one. You will find that you can vary the size of the pool by altering the size of the drop on the end of the needle.

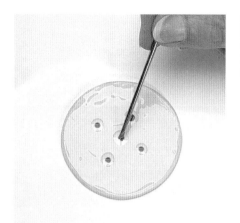 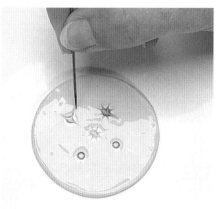 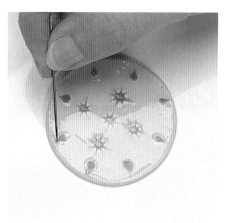

ten | Add blue drops

Mix some blue oil paint into another teaspoon of Liquid Sculpey. Apply drops of this to the centers of each of the outer pools of white. Repeat with magenta for the central pool. Use the same technique of lifting the needle so that the thread of color parts vertically above the application point. If you take the needle sideways as you lift, the thread will make a trail to one side and spoil the effect. The drops of color will form perfect circles within the pools of white.

eleven | Create stars

Finally, apply another smaller drop of white in the center of each colored pool. To make the stars, draw the pointed tip of a darning needle from the center of each pool outward. Work round each star, pulling out eight points on each. It is easier to do this evenly by working in pairs—pull out the top and bottom points, then the two sides, then the points between.

twelve | Create hearts

To make the hearts, drop pools of white at regular intervals around the edge of the lid. Then drop in pools of violet. Draw the darning needle right through the center of each pool, starting on the side toward the center and ending at the edge of the lid. This will form a perfect heart!

thirteen | Bake and finish

Bake the box lid on the tile for 20 minutes. When cool, attach the lid insert centrally to the underside of the lid with Fun-Tak. Push the lid onto the box to check the fit, adjust if necessary, and mark the position with a pencil. Glue in place with superglue.

Other Suggestions |

Try making boxes using different pearl clay colors—here silver and pearl clay are mixed to make a pale silver powder box. The lines of white and purple dots on the powder box lid were applied after baking the main Liquid Sculpey decoration. With the tapestry needle loaded with white or purple Liquid Sculpey, touch the needle down in a line of dots—each dot will be smaller than the previous one and they will remain raised on the surface. Bake again for 30 minutes.

Art Nouveau Frame

Art Nouveau style was popular in the Western world during the late nineteenth and early twentieth centuries. It developed as a reaction against the oppressive opulence of Victorian design and was based on images from nature with flowing, simple lines. This little frame, in simulated silver cloisonné enamel, is typical of the designs of that period. Its cool colors and iris motif would show off any favorite photograph to perfection.

Epoxy or cold enamels are used to give the glassy transparent pools of color in this project. See pages 10–11 for details of this material.

materials>

> 2-ounce (60g) blocks of polymer clay: 1 black
> tracing paper and pencil
> two ceramic tiles
> darning needle
> tissue blade
> silver powder
> gloss varnish
> paintbrush
> Envirotex Lite, Crystal Sheen or Epoxy (cold) enamels (see page 10)
> transparent epoxy colors: blue, green, amber (or use tiny amounts of oil paint)
> mixing cups
> tile or palette to mix on
> tapestry needle
> shoebox to cover the frame while the enamel sets
> acetate sheet (optional)
> superglue
> black carpet tape or masking tape
> thick cardstock
> heavy-duty craft knife
> metal straightedge

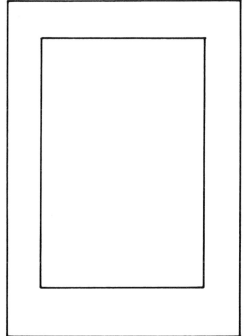

Enlarge to 125% to bring pattern to original size.

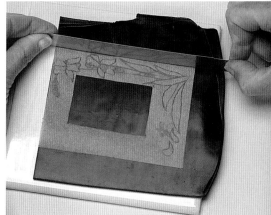

one | Preparation

Trace the frame front onto tracing paper and the frame back onto thin cardstock. Cut these out to make templates.

two | Make the frame front

Roll the black clay into a sheet about ³⁄₃₂" (2mm) thick and place it on a tile. Lay the frame front tracing on the clay and scribe over the outline of the design with a darning needle to impress the lines onto the clay surface.

three | Trim excess clay

Cut around the outside of the template with a tissue blade and remove the waste clay from around the frame. The frame will not be removed from the tile until after baking to avoid distorting it.

four | Cut corners neatly

Cut out the frame opening using your knife. To cut the corners neatly, first position the point of your knife precisely on the corner and cut by drawing your knife along the line away from the corner, stopping before you reach the opposite corner.

five | Repeat

Repeat to make a cut from the same corner along the other cutting line. Cut all the corners in this way, always cutting from a corner outward.

six | Remove clay

Remove the rectangle of waste clay from the inside of the frame opening by digging into it with your knife and then lifting it away. Be careful not to damage the edges of the frame opening as you do this.

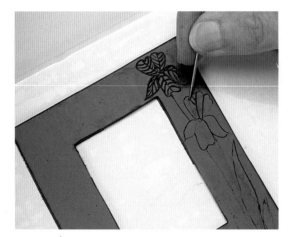

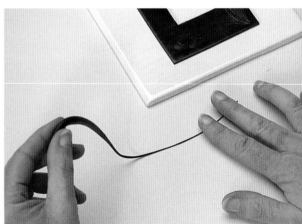

seven | Decorate the frame front

Remove the tracing and use the blunt point of a tapestry needle to scribe along the lines of the design to make them clearer. Use the point to mark textural lines on the petals and leaves, using the template as a guide. These lines will show through the transparent cold enamel and add texture to the design.

eight | Create a thin clay thread

Roll out a thin thread of clay to use for the cloisonné outline. See page 15 for instructions on how to roll thin threads of clay with a handle of thicker clay for controlling the thread. The thread should be about 1/32" (1mm) thick.

nine | Apply the clay thread

Holding the thread by its handle of thicker clay, lay it along one of the lines of the design. Use your knife to push the thread into position and trim it to length. The clay handle saves you from touching the fine thread with warm hands and distorting it. Roll out more threads of clay and apply to all the outline lines of the design in the same way.

ten | Press down the clay threads

Press the threads down lightly with your finger. Each petal or leaf must be completely enclosed with a thread of clay so that when the colored enamel is applied, it cannot flow out. The threads also need to be in contact with the clay surface of the frame all along their lengths or the enamel may seep underneath them.

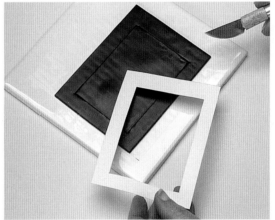

eleven | Brush with silver powder

Brush the frame with silver powder so that the black clay is completely covered. Try not to lift any of the threads as you brush. If any do lift up, gently push them back into place. After baking, they will be consolidated by the coat of varnish.

twelve | Cut out the frame back

Roll out another sheet of clay on a second tile and cut out the frame back in the same way as the frame front. Cut out around the central opening, but leave the clay in place until after the frame back is baked. This central section will become the removable part of the frame back that allows you to insert or change the photograph. Bake the frame front and back on their respective tiles for 30 to 40 minutes.

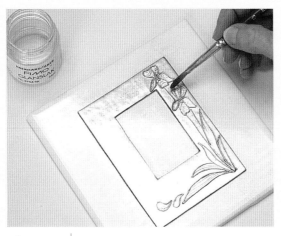

thirteen | Varnish

When the frame front has cooled, varnish the whole front to seal the silver powder. Be sure that you do not miss any parts of the design because loose powder will float to the top of the epoxy enamel when it is applied and spoil the transparency.

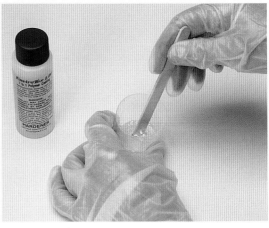

fourteen | Mix epoxy

Using gloves for hand protection, mix the epoxy according to the manufacturer's instructions. This is usually equal parts of epoxy and hardener or in the ratio of 1 part hardener to 2 parts epoxy. Stir thoroughly and set aside for a few minutes to allow the air bubbles to disperse.

fifteen | Tint epoxy

Pour about half a teaspoonful of the epoxy enamel mixture onto a tile. Use the tapestry needle to mix in a little transparent blue color and stir thoroughly. The color should be fairly strong but should not lose its transparency. It will set without any color change.

sixteen | Apply epoxy to frame

Use the tapestry needle to drop pools of blue epoxy enamel into each iris petal cell. The layer should be thick enough to reach almost to the top of the clay thread surrounding the petal shape. Push the enamel into the corners with the point of your needle.

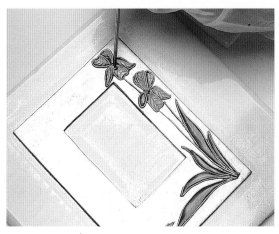

seventeen | Cure overnight

Repeat for all the other shapes, dropping green enamel into the leaves and a touch of orange into the iris centers. Place the completed frame front on a level surface, cover with an upturned shoebox to protect it from dust and leave overnight to cure.

eighteen | Assemble the frame

Glue the frame front to the frame back with superglue, matching the outside edges all around. Cut your chosen photograph so that it is slightly smaller than the frame back insert. If you want to use acetate sheet as glass, cut this to the same size.

nineteen | Attach the frame back

Lay the acetate (if used), then the photograph into the rebate in the back of the frame. Push on the frame back insert and tape the joins with black carpet tape. This means that you can change the photograph if you wish.

twenty | Create frame stand

Trace the frame stand onto thick cardstock and cut out using a metal rule and a heavy-duty craft knife. Score along the dotted line and turn the stand over so the scoring is toward the frame. Tape the top of the stand to the frame back, 1¼" (3cm) from the top of the frame. Bend the stand outward to prop the frame.

Pomanders make lovely presents and this little pomander has a distinctly Elizabethan flavor with its simple flower cutouts, golden cord and antique bronze finish. It is designed to hang in a closet or on a coat hanger to fragrance clothes.

I have used a potato, carved into a heart shape, as a former. You could try carving potatoes into other simple shapes as well: Stars or teardrops, for example, would make delightful pomanders!

materials>

> 2-ounce (60g) blocks of polymer clay: 1 black and small scraps for the leaf stamp

> talcum powder

> medium-size potato (about 3" to 4" [7.5 to 10cm] long)

> sharp vegetable knife

> foil

> teaspoon

> sharp scissors and craft knife

> selection of small flower cutters, the largest ⅜" (10mm) or less

> Super Bronze Pearl Ex powder

> stiff cardstock (card)

> 6" (15cm) square piece of red-brown silk fabric

> 8" (20cm) thick gold cord

> 12" (30cm) peach silk ribbon, ⅜" (10mm) wide

> PVA glue

> potpourri (coarse is best)

one | Make the leaf stamp

Form a ⅛" (3mm) ball of scrap clay and shape it into a
teardrop. Press it onto a tile to flatten it and mark veins with
your knife. Bake for 15 minutes. When cool, form a ¼" (6mm)
thick log of scrap clay, about 1" (2.5cm) long, cut off one end
and pinch it into a similar shaped cross-section as the baked
leaf. Brush the leaf with talcum powder and press the shaped
end of the log onto it to take an impression. Bake the stamp for
30 minutes.

two | Cut the potato in half

Cut off the ends of the potato and then cut it in half lengthwise
so that it has a flat back. Lay it down on your work surface. It
needs to be about 2½" (6cm) tall, the same across and about 1"
(2.5 cm) thick.

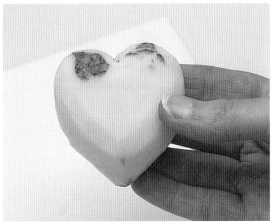

three | Shape the potato former

Looking down on the potato from above, cut it into a heart
shape by trimming the bottom into a point and cutting a notch
in the center top. Trim the sides into smooth curves.

four | Round cut edges

Round the cut edges to make all the curves gentle. The resulting shape should be domed with no undercuts so that after the
clay has been shaped and baked on it, the potato former can be
removed easily.

five | Cover potato with foil

Cover the potato heart with foil and smooth down well, turning the edges of the foil to the back of the potato. Use the back of a teaspoon to smooth the foil down firmly.

six | Cover with a sheet of clay

Roll out a sheet of black clay, about ³⁄₃₂" (2mm) thick and lay this over the heart shape. Press the clay down all around, coaxing it into a smooth curve over the top of the heart and tucking it down the sides without any folds.

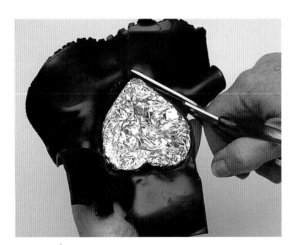

seven | Trim excess clay

Turn the heart over and use a pair of scissors to trim the clay around the edge of the heart. Make sure that the clay does not fold over onto the back of the heart or it will be impossible to remove it from the potato after baking.

eight | Cut hole for hanging cord

Use the point of your knife to cut out a circle of clay from the top of the heart. This will provide the hole for the hanging cord and should be wide enough to take the cord doubled.

nine | Cut out clay shapes

Brush over the surface of the clay with talcum powder. This will prevent the cutters and stamp from sticking to the clay. Use the flower cutters to cut out a pattern of flower shapes in the clay. Press each cutter down hard onto the clay and remove the cutout piece. Do not cut out too many shapes or the clay will be weakened.

ten | Add leaf impressions

Stamp leaf impressions between the cutout flowers with the leaf stamp. Angle the leaves as though they were radiating from the flowers. This will add to the texture of the pomander for the effect of worked metal.

eleven | Apply bronze powder

Dip your fingertip into the bronze powder and brush it over the surface of the pomander. This highlights the raised areas and leaves the stamped details black to suggest antique metalwork.

twelve | Bake and remove potato

Bake the pomander on the potato for at least 45 to 50 minutes. The potato inside the foil will keep the clay cooler, so it needs a long time to be thoroughly baked. Allow the potato to cool completely, then open the back of the foil and scoop out the potato until you can remove it all and the foil from inside the pomander. If the clay shows any signs of cracking, it is not baked enough and should be returned to the oven for another 30 minutes.

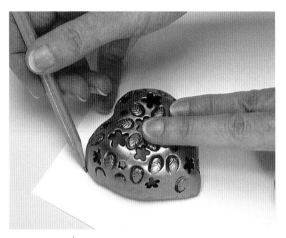

thirteen | Varnish and trace

Varnish the pomander to protect the bronze powder and allow it to dry. Place the pomander on the thick cardstock and draw around it.

fourteen | Cut out card heart

Draw a second line about ½" (13mm) inside the heart outline. Cut out the card heart and cut out the inner heart. This makes a frame to stretch fabric over for a permeable backing for the pomander. The fabric will allow the fragrance from the potpourri to pass through.

fifteen | Cut out fabric heart

Place the card heart, with the pencil markings still upward, onto the wrong side of the fabric. Draw around it with a pen and then draw another line about ¼" (6mm) outside the first. Cut out the fabric heart along this outer line.

sixteen | Cut notches in fabric

Lay the card heart, with the pencil markings still upward, back on the fabric heart. Cut notches around the edge of the fabric so that it can be folded over onto the card without having to make creases.

seventeen | Glue together

Apply PVA glue all around the card and press the fabric over onto it, stretching the fabric slightly to make a smooth finish. Allow the glue to dry.

eighteen | Add cord

Fold the gold cord in half and push the cut ends through the hole in the top of the pomander. Glue down the ends inside the pomander with PVA glue and allow to dry.

nineteen | Add potpourri

Fill the pomander with coarse potpourri. Give it a little shake so that any fine particles fall out through the holes in the front. You can then fill it with more coarse pieces. Squeeze a line of PVA glue along the back edge of the pomander and press on the fabric-covered card back, raw edges to the inside.

twenty | Cover join with ribbon

Starting at the top where the cord emerges, glue the ribbon all around the sides of the pomander, covering the join between the card and the clay. Glue the ends down neatly. PVA glue is removable from clay, so when the fragrance from the potpourri fades, you can open the back of the pomander to refill it.

))) **WILLIAM MORRIS ONCE** *declared:*
"Have nothing in your houses that you do not know
to be useful, or believe to be beautiful." This is a
saying true to my own heart. I feel that it is surely a

bonus if you can fill your house with items that are both useful

the kitchen

and beautiful!

THE PROJECTS IN THIS *chapter all follow this*
idea. The jug cover is useful but will also add a crisp delicacy to
a jug of lemonade, while the fridge magnets will hold messages
on your refrigerator but should bring a touch of gaiety as they do
so. Finally, the switchplate cover will transform an everyday
necessity into a dreamy mosaic.

Teapot Fridge Magnets

Tea drinking is a British institution and most British homes will have a homely teapot for everyday use, as well as a fine teapot for special occasions. This little trio of fridge magnets has a typical homely brown teapot, a light blue teapot in the elegant style that Wedgwood made famous, and a Georgian style teapot that would probably have been handed down as a family heirloom!

The "Wedgwood" teapot uses a polymer clay appliqué technique of applying tiny slices of clay to suggest a cameo effect. A curved knife blade like the one shown in the photographs is the best to use for this.

"Wedgwood" teapot

Homely teapot

"Georgian" teapot

materials>

All teapots
) ceramic tile to work on
) large tapestry needle and craft knife
) magnetic strip or small magnets
) superglue

Homely teapot
) 2-ounce (60g) blocks of polymer clay: ¼ block of beige (Premo Ecru)
) artist's soft pastel: brown
) soft paintbrush

"Wedgwood" teapot
) 2-ounce (60g) blocks of polymer clay: ¼ block of light blue and a small quantity each of translucent and white
) brush protector or smooth, round pencil
) craft knife with a curved blade
) fine tapestry needle

"Georgian" teapot
) 2-ounce (60g) blocks of polymer clay: ⅛ block of white, ⅛ block of translucent
) denatured alcohol (methylated spirits)
) acrylic paint: red, green, gold
) fine paintbrush
) gloss varnish

mixtures>
) porcelain = 1 part translucent + 1 part white

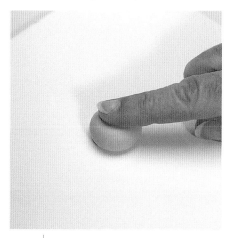

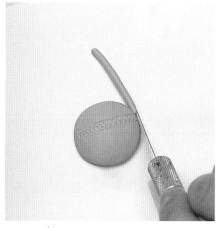

one | **Make a domed disk**

Form a ⅞" (22mm) ball of beige clay and flatten it with the pad of your finger onto the tile to make a domed disk, about 1¼" (3cm) in diameter.

two | **Decorate**

Use the eye of the tapestry needle to mark a row of impressions across the disk, about ½" (13mm) from the top. Turn the needle the other way and mark another row just below the first. This simulates the rolled decoration sometimes seen on this old-fashioned type of country teapot.

three | **Make the handle**

Form a 1⁄16" (1.5mm) thick log of beige clay, 1½" (4cm) long. Press one end of the log firmly against the side of the teapot, just above the decorated band. The rest of the log should lie pointing upward.

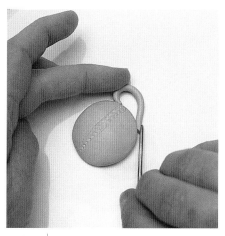

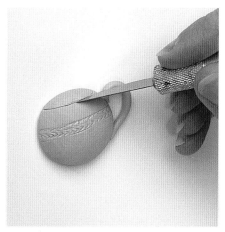

four | **Attach firmly**

Ease the top end of the log around and down in a gentle curve to make the handle. Use the tip of the tapestry needle to press the bottom end firmly against the side, just above the base of the teapot.

five | **Make the lid**

Mark a horizontal line with your knife blade across the top of the teapot to suggest a lid. This should be parallel to the band of decoration and about 3⁄16" (5mm) from the top of the teapot.

six | **Make the spout**

Form a ⅜" (10mm) ball of clay and roll it into a tapered log, 1⅛" (28mm) long, for the spout. Cut off the thick end at an angle so that the spout will fit neatly against the curved side of the teapot.

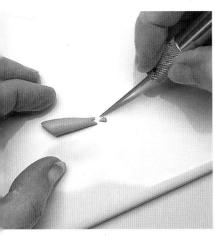

seven | Notch spout

Cut a V-shaped notch out of the pointed end for the tip of the spout. This type of decorative spout is reputed to stop drips!

eight | Attach spout

Press the cut end of the spout against the lower left-hand side of the teapot body. Curve the spout upward and then bend the tip down slightly to make an attractive shape. Press a tiny ball of clay onto the top of the lid for the lid knob.

nine | Brown the pot

Rub some brown artist's pastel onto a piece of paper. Use a soft brush to scoop up some of the resulting powder and brush it onto the teapot to suggest a glaze. Brush a thicker layer onto the decorated band, the lid, the base of the teapot, the top of the handle and the spout tip.

))) "Wedgwood" Teapot

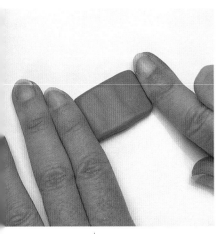

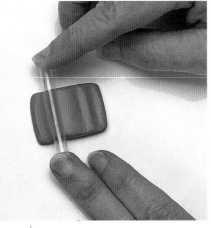

one | Make body

Form a ⅞" (22mm) ball of light blue clay and roll it into a cylinder, ⅝" (15mm) thick and 1⅛" (28mm) long. Press this down on a tile to flatten it into a rectangle, 1¼" (3cm) across and 1" (2.5cm) tall for the teapot body. Keep pushing the sides inward as you flatten the clay to keep the rectangular shape.

two | Groove teapot body

Press the side of a brush protector (or smooth pencil) onto the clay to make shallow vertical grooves on the teapot body. Group two grooves together at each side and leave the central section smooth to suggest the ridged effect of a classic teapot.

three | Make the lid

Form a ³⁄₁₆" (5mm) ball of light blue clay and shape this into a short log, tapered at each end and about ¾" (20mm) long. Press onto the top of the teapot for the lid. Mark the bottom of the log with the side of a tapestry needle to suggest the sides of the lid.

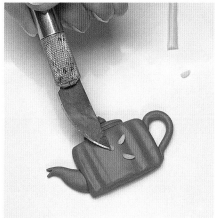

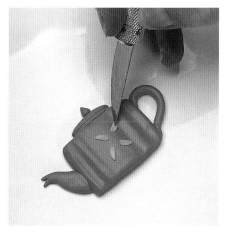

four | Add handle and spout

Make a handle and spout in the same way as for the Homely Teapot above. To make the lid knob, form a ¹⁄₁₆" (1.5mm) ball of light blue clay and shape it into a teardrop. Press this onto the top of the lid with the point upward, pinching the point with your fingertips to accentuate it as you press it down.

five | Create porcelain log for appliqué

Form a ¹⁄₁₆" (1.5mm) thick log of the porcelain mixture clay. Flatten the log slightly so that it has an oval leaf-shaped cross section. Cut off and discard the end. Cut a thin slice from the log with the tip of your knife and lift it onto the blade. Turn the blade over with the slice still sticking to it and press it onto the teapot where it will stick to the soft clay.

six | Apply leaf slices

Apply four leaf slices in this way, radiating outward from the center of the teapot. Mark veins on the leaves with your knife blade.

seven | Add flower petals

Roll the porcelain log to make it thinner and give it a round cross section. Cut and apply slices for the flower petals. Arrange the petals in groups of five, radiating from a central point for each flower. Make three flowers, two at the top and one below, their petals overlapping the leaves.

eight | Accentuate centers

Pierce the center of each flower with the blunt point of the large tapestry needle. This accentuates the flowers' centers.

nine | Add flowers

Form a log of porcelain, about ¹⁄₃₂" (1mm) thick. Cut and apply slices of this for lines of tiny flowers arching outward from the top and bottom of the bouquet.

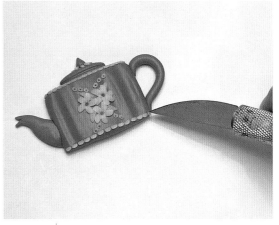

ten | Add more detail

Pierce the center of each tiny flower with the fine tapestry needle. This is an easy way to make tiny and delicate appliqué flowers—piercing the center cups each slice into a flower shape.

eleven | Decorate top and bottom

Flatten the ⅓₂" (1mm) log into an oval cross section and cut slices to apply all along the top and bottom of the teapot. Always apply each slice with the same side upward so that all the slices look identical in shape. Apply a ring of slices radiating from the the lid knob.

twelve | Bake and add magnet

Bake the teapots on their tiles for 20 to 30 minutes. When cool, glue a ½" (13mm) length of magnetic strip to the back of each teapot with superglue.

Georgian teapot |

The white and gold teapot in the photograph is made in a similar way to the homely teapot using porcelain mixture clay. The sides are pushed inward on the tile to shape them into an elegant curve. The teapot is then indented with a tapestry needle to suggest fluting. After baking, brush over the teapot with denatured alcohol (methylated spirits) to degrease the surface and paint a design in acrylic paint with a fine paintbrush. Finally, varnish the teapot with gloss varnish.

Lemon Beaded Jug Cover >*project two*

Dainty beaded jug covers were popular in the Victorian kitchen—and on the tea table as well. Here is a polymer clay version with little lemons added to the beads to make a pretty jug cover for lemonade, lemon tea or any favorite drink.

Besides looking extremely pretty on a table, jug covers are useful for outdoor occasions—the beaded edging holds the cover down so that the breeze will not blow it away and rose petals cannot drift into the lemonade!

materials>

> 2-ounce (60g) blocks of polymer clay: ½ block of lemon yellow and a small amount of leaf green
> ½ yard (45cm) lace fabric or tulle
> 8" (20cm) diameter plate
> pencil
> Fray Check
> 1 yard (90cm) of ½" (13mm) wide edging lace with points about every inch
> needle and white thread
> darning needle
> toothbrush
> ¾ ounce (20g) clear transparent seed beads
> about 20 small green transparent seed beads
> needle and strong white thread for stringing the beads
> craft knife
> tile (optional)

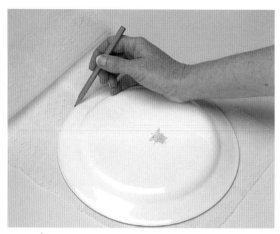

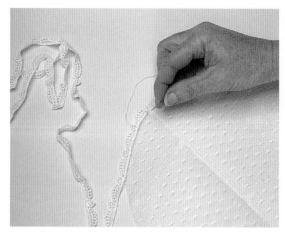

Bead Number

Count the number of points on the lace edging—you will need this number of small yellow beads and half the number of lemon beads.

one | Cut circle of fabric

Lay the plate upside-down on the lace fabric and draw around the outside with a pencil to make a circle. Cut out the fabric just inside the pencil line and treat the edge with Fray Check to stop it from fraying if necessary.

two | Sew lace onto fabric circle

Cut a length of lace to go around the outside of the fabric circle with an overlap of ½" (13mm) where the ends join. Lay the lace around the edge of the fabric circle, covering the raw edge of the fabric by about ¼" (6mm), and sew it neatly to the fabric with small stitches.

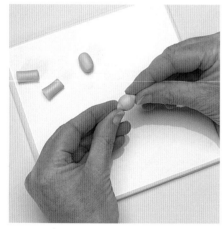

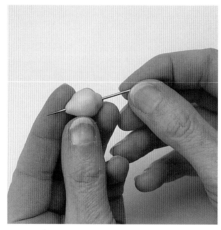

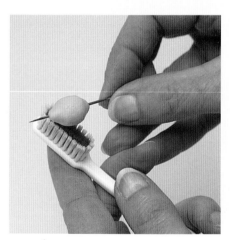

three | Make lemon beads

Form the yellow clay into a log, ⅜" (10mm) thick and about 6" (15cm) long. Cut ½" (13mm) lengths for the lemon beads. Form a length into a ball, then shape it into an oval. Pinch all around each end with your thumb and forefinger to make a lemon shape.

four | Pierce the beads

Pierce through the pointed ends of the lemon with the darning needle. Holding the bead on the darning needle, roll it from side to side on your palm to even it up. This will enlarge the hole as well.

five | Texture the lemons

With the darning needle still piercing the lemon, hold the lemon against the bristles of the toothbrush and roll it across the bristles to texture it.

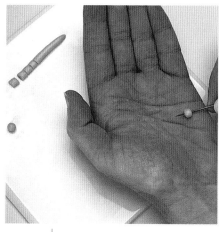

six | Add leaves

Form a ⅛" (3mm) ball of leaf green clay and shape it into a small leaf following the instructions on page 27. Slice it off the work surface and press it onto one end of the lemon. Repeat steps 3 to 6 to make all the other lemon beads.

seven | Make small beads

To make the small yellow beads, form a ¼" (6mm) thick log of yellow clay and cut it into ⅛" (3mm) thick slices. Roll each of these into a ball and pierce it with the darning needle. Roll the side of the bead against your palm to even it up, in the same way as for the lemons. Lay all the beads on a cookie sheet lined with baking parchment and bake for 20 to 30 minutes.

eight | Make the bead fringe

Knot the end of a double length of strong white thread and anchor it to one of the lace points with a couple of stitches. Thread on ten transparent beads, then a small yellow bead and then ten more transparent beads. Check that this is long enough to reach to the next point in a gentle curve and, if not, adjust the number of transparent beads. Anchor the thread with a stitch at the next point. Repeat for the second loop of beads.

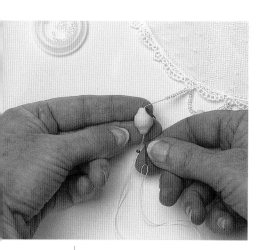

nine | Make the lemon dangles

Thread on ten transparent beads, then a lemon bead from the top (leaf end) down, then thread on a transparent green bead. Now take your needle and thread back up through the lemon.

ten | Finish the assembly

Finally take your needle back up through the ten transparent beads again. Pull up and anchor the thread. Continue around the cover in this way, alternating two loops of small beads with a lemon dangle. When you have worked around the cover, you may need to insert an extra beaded loop if the number of points is not even. Fasten off firmly with a few small stitches. The jug cover can be hand washed gently by squeezing in soapy water.

Variations

Try making tiny orange or strawberry beads instead of lemons.

Mountain Lake Switchplate

This project is in the style of Pietre Dure, a beautiful Italian mosaic technique that uses shapes cut from semiprecious stones to make a picture. True Pietre Dure pieces are rare and costly, but this polymer clay version is not difficult to achieve and gives an effect very like the real thing!

The misty beauty of Lake Wallowa in Oregon inspired the mountain lake image for this project. My kitchen often becomes far too hot, and having this cool vision on the wall transports me to a wonderful place.

A standard plastic United States switchplate cover is used for this project and can be baked safely. Switchplate shapes vary between countries, so you will have to adapt the design if you have a different shape of cover.

materials>

) 2-ounce (60g) blocks of polymer clay: 1 translucent; ¼ block each of blue, black, dark brown, blue-green, leaf green; and small amounts of white, purple, golden yellow, orange, gold and pearl

) plastic switchplate cover

) pasta machine or roller and wood strips

) tracing paper and pencil

) darning needle

) talcum powder and soft paintbrush for brushing on the talc

) craft knife and tissue blade

) brush protector or round cutter to fit the screw holes

) sandpaper and quilt wadding

) Liquid Sculpey or PVA glue

) acrylic paint: pale blue and dark blue

mixtures>

All the following should be mixed until lightly marbled:

) sky blue: 1" (2.5cm) ball of translucent + ¼" (6mm) ball of blue

) sky light grey: 1" (2.5cm) ball of translucent + ¼" (6mm) ball of black

) light purple: ¾" (20mm) ball of translucent + ⅛" (3mm) ball of purple

) dark green: ½" (13mm) ball blue-green + ½" (13mm) ball black

) pale green: ¾" (20mm) ball of translucent + ⅛" (3mm) ball of dark green

) lake blue: ¾" (20mm) ball of blue + ¾" (20mm) ball of translucent + ¼" (6mm) ball of pearl

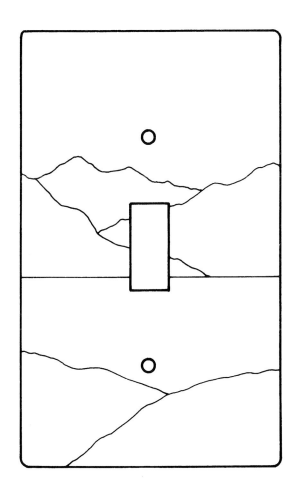

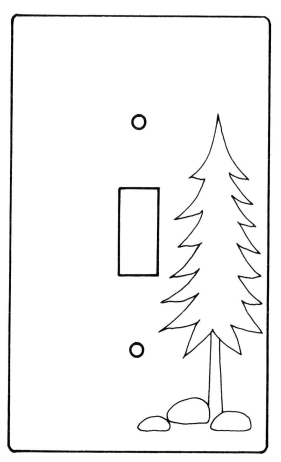

Switchplate pattern is full-size.

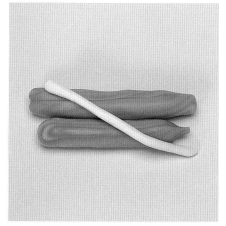

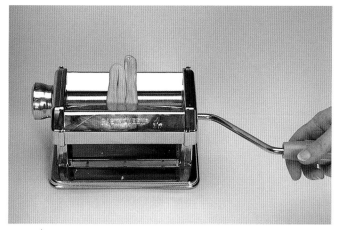

one | Make marbled logs

Roll the marbled sky blue and sky light grey clays into ½" (13mm) thick logs and press together with a ⅛" (3mm) thick log of white. Roll all together to make a longer log, fold in half and roll again. Repeat this until the clay is marbled with streaks of white (see page 18).

two | Make marble sheets for sky

Set the pasta machine to a medium setting and keep it at this setting throughout the project so that all sheets are the same thickness. Form the marbled log into an S-shape and roll through the pasta machine, placing the side of the S in the machine first. This will give loops and horizontal lines to suggest swirling clouds for the sky. If you are not happy with the result, fold the sheet in half and pass through the pasta machine again for more swirls.

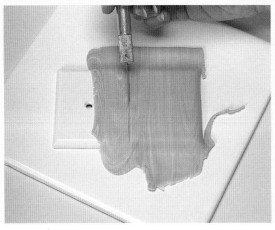

three | Cut out sky

Choose an attractive part of the sheet and lay this onto the top half of the switchplate cover. Trim around the outside and press down gently all over so that it sticks well to the cover, smoothing out any bubbles.

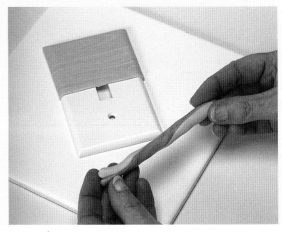

four | Marble log for mountain

Trim the bottom of the sky along a horizontal line across the center of the switchplate cover. Marble the light purple mixture with the remains of the sky color to make a pale streaky purple that tones with the sky. Pass through the pasta machine longitudinally in the direction of the streaks.

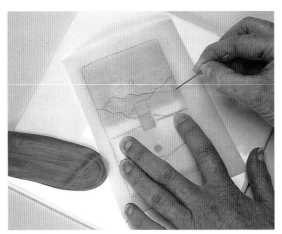

five | Mark spot for mountain

Trace the background template onto tracing paper and lay this over the switchplate cover. Scribe along the lines of the furthest mountain with the darning needle, continuing the lines downward to the edges of the plate across the near mountains.

six | Remove mountain pattern

Cut along the scribed lines and carefully remove the piece—do not squash it, as this is now your pattern to cut out the mountain.

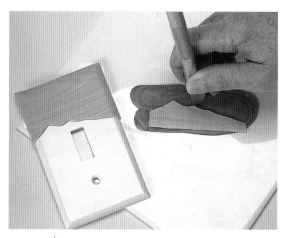

seven | Cut out mountain shape

Brush the surface of the light purple sheet with talcum powder to prevent sticking. Lay the cutout mountain shape onto the sheet with the marbled streaks horizontal. Cut around it as accurately as possible, holding your knife vertically.

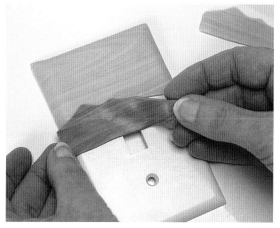

eight | Add mountain shape

Press the purple cutout mountain shape into the space on the cover, matching the curves and smoothing in the edges. Avoid stretching the clay, and the mountain should fit exactly into the space.

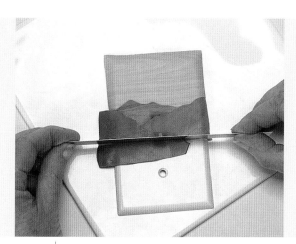

nine | Make the near mountain

Repeat the scribing and cutting-out to insert the near mountains. Use pale green marbled with an equal quantity of the remaining light purple for the right-hand mountain, and add a trace of dark green to this mixture for the left-hand mountain. Each time, roll out the clay in the direction of the streaks and angle the streaks down into the center of the picture when you cut out each shape to create a feeling of depth. Trim horizontally across the bottom of the mountains for the lake surface.

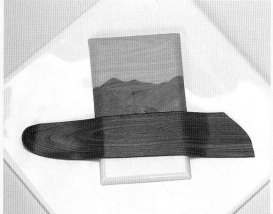

ten | Make the lake

Form a log of the lake blue marbled clay, fold it in half and roll out in the direction of the streaks as before. Cut a straight edge along one edge of this sheet and butt this against the bottom of the mountains. Trim the sides. There is no need for the blue to reach the bottom of the switchplate because this will be covered with foreground.

eleven | Marble foreground log

Lightly marble together logs made from ½" (13mm) balls of leaf green, dark brown, golden yellow and orange. Cut ⅛" (3mm) thick slices from the resulting log, which should show a mottled cross section. Lay the slices tightly together to make a continuous mat, then pass this through the pasta machine to make a mottled green sheet for the two foreground pieces.

twelve | Cut out left foreground

Scribe and cut out the left foreground in the same way as the left near mountains. This will only give you a part pattern because the lake blue clay does not reach the bottom of the switchplate. Use the tracing to fill in the rest of the shape when cutting the piece from the mottled green sheet.

thirteen | Create right foreground pattern

Scribe and cut out the right foreground area. Again, this may give only a part pattern, but you can fill in the remainder by eyeballing it or use the tracing as a guide to the bottom of the shape.

fourteen | Cut out right foreground

Lay the cutout pattern on the remaining mottled green sheet and cut around it for the right foreground. Try to angle any streaks differently from the left foreground so that there will be a line between the two foregrounds.

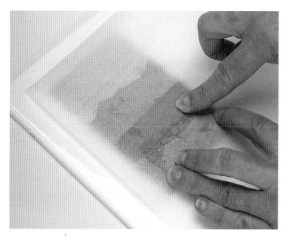

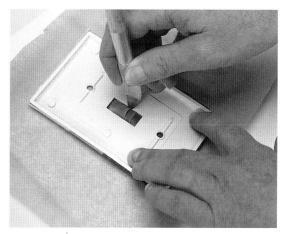

fifteen | Smooth the surface

Lay a sheet of tracing paper over the switchplate cover and burnish with your finger to smooth the surface. The translucent paper will allow you to see if there are any dips or air bubbles that need smoothing.

sixteen | Cut switch hole and bake

Lay the switchplate face down on nonstick baking parchment. Cut neatly around the central switch hole and use the brush protector or round cutter to cut out the screw holes. Trim around the outside of the plate and smooth away any bumps. Bake the whole plate for 20 to 30 minutes. When cool, hold under a gently running tap and sand away any rough areas. Buff the surface with quilt wadding.

seventeen | Make the tree and rocks

Form ⅜" (10mm) balls of dark green, leaf green, dark brown and black. Roll these into logs and marble until well streaked. Press the marbled log onto your work surface to flatten it a little and cut ⅛" (3mm) thick slices to make a mat as for the foreground. Cutting from a flattened log will give you a streaky mottled clay. Pass the mat through the pasta machine in the direction of the streaks.

eighteen | Cut the sheet and join

Cut the streaky mottled sheet in half along a diagonal, flip one side over, press the two halves together and smooth the join. The streaks will now join at an angle to make a chevron for the fir tree foliage.

nineteen | Cut out tree shape

Trace the tree template and lay the tracing onto the chevron sheet, aligning the center line with the center of the tree. Score along the lines with the needle and cut out the shape.

twenty | Apply tree shape

Brush a thin coat of Liquid Sculpey (or PVA glue) onto the area where the tree is to be placed. Apply the tree shape and press down. It should be raised above the background. Marble together small quantities of black, dark brown and gold clay, then roll out along the streaks for the trunk.

twenty-one | Add more details

Cut a strip from the brown sheet for the trunk and apply at the base of the tree foliage. Marble together the scraps from the mountains with some sky grey clay to make a mottled grey log for the rocks. Taper the log and cut slices of different sizes from different points along it to make different-sized rocks. Apply these around the base of the tree. Use a smear of Liquid Sculpey to help them stick.

twenty-two | Bake and trim

Bake the switchplate again for 20 minutes. When it is cool, cut away any excess clay around the screw holes so that the screws will lie flush. Paint the heads of the screws with acrylic paint to match the background colors. Screw the switchplate into place on the wall.

Variation |

The Pietre Dure technique can be adapted to make beautiful boxes; here, an Italian lake scene is used for a box lid. The sides and base of the box are made from black clay sheets, backed with a marbled clay layer and then baked and glued together. The Pietre Dure lid is made on a ceramic tile, baked, then backed with marbled clay and rebaked. Finally, a baked clay box lid insert is glued to the back of the lid for a snug fit.

))) POLYMER CLAY IS IDEAL *for making lasting items for your home, but it is also perfect for seasonal decorations. Unlike less durable items, you can store away the polymer clay*

holiday decorations

decorations after the holiday with no fear that they will be crushed or spoiled by the time you need them again.

TRANSLUCENT AND LIQUID POLYMER *clay can be used to make wonderful lamps and candleholders and is therefore the perfect material for exciting Halloween decorations. You could adapt the ideas in the projects to make many other kinds of candle lamps. Finally, frosty white clays are combined with pearly powders to simulate icy winter snowflakes and icicles that can be made in all shapes and sizes for a sparkling winter holiday display!*

) haunted house candle lamp > p. 116 　　　) winter snowflakes & icicles > p. 120

>*project one* # Haunted House Candle Lamp

This little house is great fun to make! The walls are sheets of black polymer clay and the brightly lit windows are tinted Transparent Liquid Sculpey. A black cat prowls on the roof next to the crazy crooked chimney. Templates are provided for you to cut out the house shapes, but you could have fun designing your own—a row of candlelit crooked houses on a windowsill would make a wonderful Halloween display. Use strong clay for this project and bake the pieces well.

materials>

> 2-ounce (60g) block of polymer clay: 1 black

> tracing paper and pencil

> scissors

> three ceramic tiles at least 6" (15cm) square

> brush protector or ¼" (6mm) round cutter

> blunt tapestry needle

> Transparent Liquid Sculpey

> oil paint: red, yellow, green, blue

> superglue

> roller

> craft knife

> votive candle and small jar to hold it

Enlarge pattern to 133%
to bring to full size.

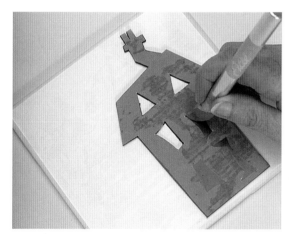

one | Cut out the house shapes

Trace the three house pieces from the template and cut them out. Roll out a sheet of black clay, about 1⁄16" (1.5mm) thick, and place on a tile. Lay the house front tracing on the sheet and cut out the house front. Cut out the window shapes neatly with the point of your knife and pull out the waste clay.

two | Cut a scalloped edge

Use the brush protector to cut a scalloped edge along the bottom edges of the roof. Hold the brush protector at an angle and make scalloped impressions across the front of the house to continue the bottom line of the roof.

three | Detail the door

Mark the edge of the door with the tapestry needle and make a hole in the top center of the door to suggest a small, round decorative window.

four | Deatil the windows

Form a ¼" (6mm) thick log of black clay and roll one end into a thin length about ⅟₁₆" (1.5mm) thick and 2" (5cm) long. Hold the log by the thick end so that you have control and lay the thin end down the center of one of the windows. Trim it to length and press the two ends against the top and bottom of the window frame to secure them. Repeat to make a line across the window. Divide the other windows into panes in the same way.

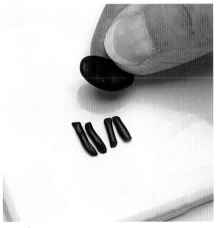

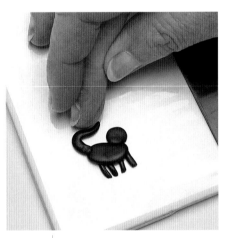

five | Make the house sides

Cut out the house sides from black clay sheets on two more tiles and cut scallops along each roof side with the brush protector. Cut out the rose window on the left house side using the brush protector. First cut out the central round pane to position the window, then cut the surrounding panes.

six | Make the cat

Form a ⅟₁₆" (1.5mm) thick log of black clay and cut four ⅜" (10mm) lengths for the cat's legs. Press these down on the tile in two pairs with a slight gap between the pairs. Form a ⅜" (10mm) ball of black and shape it into an oval. Flatten it a little and press down over the tops of the legs, angling the left side upward to suggest an arching back.

seven | Add head and tail

Flatten a ¼" (6mm) ball of black clay and press onto the right side for the head. Form a ⅟₁₆" (1.5mm) thick log, ¾" (20mm) long, and point one end for the tail. Press onto the cat's rump, curving it over its back.

eight | Detail the cat

Form two tiny cones of black and press onto the top of the head for the ears. Mark eyes and mouth with the tip of your tapestry needle. If you make holes right through the clay, the cat's eyes will light up when the candle is lit!

nine | Add the cat

Slice under the cat with your knife to free it from the tile and lift it into place on the roof of the house. Press it down firmly to attach it to the roof—the cat's feet should overlap the top of the roof for strength.

ten | Apply the Liquid Sculpey

Pour some Transparent Liquid Sculpey into a palette and use the tapestry needle to scoop it up and drip it into several of the window areas. Fill the windows fairly thickly, but do not allow the liquid to flow over the top of the logs dividing the panes.

eleven | Color and bake

For the colored windows, mix a tiny dab of oil paint into Liquid Sculpey to make a pastel color and apply as for the white windows. If you drip any Liquid Sculpey onto the surface of the house, wipe it away gently with a tissue.

Bake all three house pieces on their tiles for 45 minutes and allow to cool. The pieces need to be strong, so do not skimp on the baking! Carefully remove the pieces from the tiles. The windows will have set into a flexible translucent layer.

twelve | Assemble the house

Use superglue to glue the two sides of the house at right angles to the house front. The house will stand up securely on the three sides. Place a night-light candle or a votive in a small glass jar inside the house and enjoy the glowing windows!

! safety

Take care that the candle flame does not come into contact with the polymer clay walls of the house or they will burn. It is safest to place the candle inside a small jelly or baby food jar.

>*project two* Winter Snowflakes & Icicles

Delicate pearly snowflakes and glittering icicles make exciting winter holiday ornaments. They can be hung around the room in a sparkling shower or used to decorate a holiday tree.

Stronger polymer clays have opened up many new design possibilities and these delicate snowflakes are a delightful example. I originally designed them many years ago and was troubled with how fragile they were. Now, made with stronger clays, they can be thin and fragile-looking when in fact they are remarkably strong.

materials>

> 2-ounce (60g) blocks of polymer clay: 1 white and 1 translucent

> compass

> pencil and paper

> ruler

> tape

> small sheet of glass with the edges sanded smooth

> Pearl White Pearl Ex powder

> paintbrush

> gloss varnish

> thread for hanging

> craft knife

> tapestry needle

mixtures>

> ice white = 1 part white + 1 part translucent

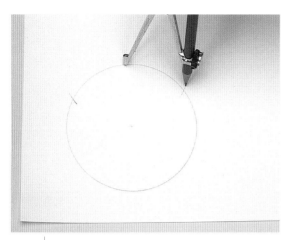

one | Make a snowflake template

To make a template for a 4" (10cm) diameter snowflake, set the compass legs 2" (5cm) apart and draw a circle on the paper. Without changing the setting, place the compass point on the circle and draw an arc cutting the line in each direction. Move the point to one of these marks and mark again, continuing around until the circle is divided into six sections.

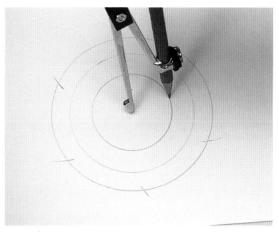

two | Add two more circles

Draw two more circles inside the first, each one about ½" (13mm) smaller in radius than the one outside it. These will help you keep the snowflake symmetrical.

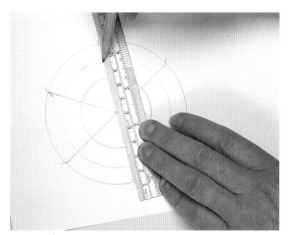

three | Mark off six arms

Lay the ruler across the center of the circle, joining opposite marks, and draw lines to give the snowflake its six arms.

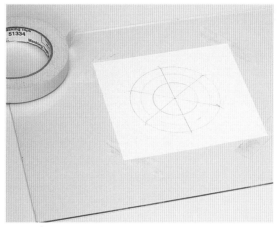

four | Ready the work space

Tape the template face down onto the sheet of glass and turn the sheet over. You can now work on the sheet of glass with the template visible through it.

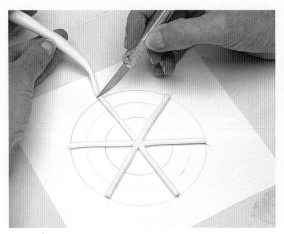

five | Make the snowflake arms

Roll the ice white clay into a log, about ⅛" (3mm) thick. Cut a 4" (10cm) length and lay this across the center of the template, on one of the lines, for the first pair of arms. Trim the ends to the outer circle. Cut four 2" (5cm) lengths from the same log for the remaining arms. Press these onto the glass along the remaining four lines with the inner end overlapping the first pair of arms enough to make a strong join.

six | Make the shorter arms

Form another log, a little thinner than the first, and apply the shorter arms of the snowflake in the same way in the spaces between the long arms. Trim these to the second circle from the outside.

seven | Create splayed ends

Cut a V shape with your knife, about ⅜" (10mm) long, in the end of each smaller arm. Push the two halves apart to make a delicate splayed end.

eight | Make the appliqué crystals

Form a ⅜" (10mm) thick log of clay. Press this down on the glass to flatten it into a strip about ½" (13mm) wide and ⅛" (3mm) thick. Cut off the end and discard it. Now cut a slice about ¹⁄₁₆" (1.5mm) thick, lifting it onto your knife blade as you cut.

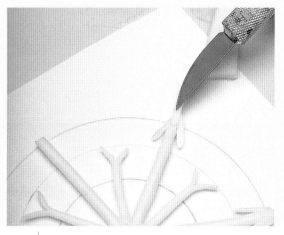

nine | Apply the crystals

Turn the knife over, with the slice still stuck to it, and press it down onto the end of one of the long arms. Repeat with a second slice to make an arrow shape. When the slice is pressed onto the clay, it will detach from the knife. This is a very useful way of applying small pieces of clay with your knife and it avoids touching them with your hands, which would distort their shape.

ten | Create a good point

Apply another slice, in the same way, straight down the end of the arm, covering the tops of the other two slices and protruding slightly beyond the end of the arm to make a good point. Repeat for all the long arms.

eleven | Create more arrow shapes

Cut and apply more slices in the same way to make further arrow shapes on the long arms. You can use your imagination here and decorate the snowflake with as many slices as you wish, but keep the pattern symmetrical.

twelve | Add to the feathery effect

Apply longer slices running in angled pairs from each shorter arm across to the longer arms on either side. Besides adding to the feathery effect, these will reinforce the snowflake and make it stronger.

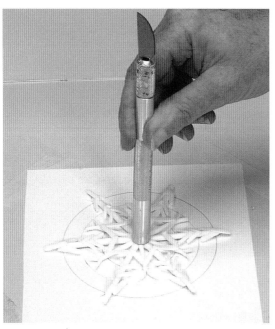

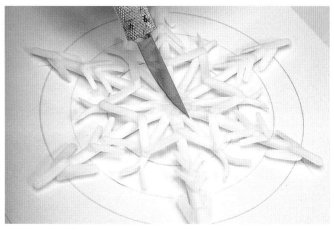

fourteen | Decorate the center

Use your knife blade to impress a pattern on the central area. Alternatively, you could use a small stamp or impress it with a star cutter.

thirteen | Strengthen the center

Press the end of a pencil or your knife handle into the center of the snowflake. This will consolidate the area where all the arms join and make it neater.

fifteen | Add pearl white powder

Brush over the snowflake with pearl white powder. Bake on the glass for 20 to 30 minutes. When cool, varnish to protect the powder. You can hang the snowflake by tying a thread to one of its arms.

Variations |

You can vary the design of your snowflakes by altering the size and the placement of the applied slices. Try dusting the snowflakes and icicles with gold, silver or other pearlescent powders for a glorious display.

sixteen | Make the icicles

Form a tapered log of ice white clay about 6" (15mm) long, ⅜" (10mm) thick at the top and tapering to a point. Flatten the top a little and make a hole with a tapestry needle so you can hang the icicle from a thread after baking.

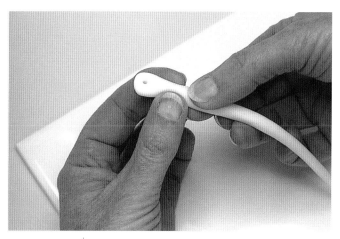

seventeen | Ripple the icicle

Place your left-hand thumb and forefinger on either side of the icicle, a little way below the flattened top, and squeeze the clay to thin the log at this point. With your left-hand still pinching the clay, place your right-hand thumb and forefinger on the front and back of the icicle and squeeze in the opposite direction. This will begin to ripple the icicle to look like real ice.

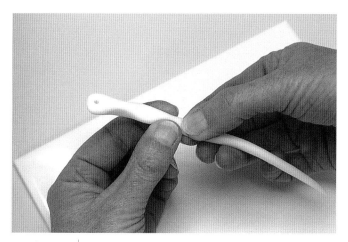

eighteen | Continue ripples

Move both hands down the icicle and repeat the pinching to make another series of indentations just below the first two, one flattening the icicle from the sides, the other from front to back. Continue all the way down to the point of the icicle in this way to make alternating indentations.

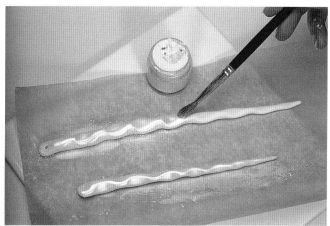

nineteen | Add powder and bake

Make several icicles of different sizes. Lay them on baking parchment and brush over with pearl white powder. Bake for 20 to 30 minutes. When cool, varnish with gloss varnish to protect the powder and make them look really icy. Tie a cord through the hole in each icicle and hang in groups for a shivery effect!

Resources

Polymer clay suppliers

Polymer clays are widely available in craft and art materials shops and also by mail order from craft suppliers. If you have problems finding the clays, the following suppliers should be able to help.

))) Australia

Rossdale Pty Ltd
137 Noone Street
Clifton Hills VIC 3068
001 613 9482 3988
E-mail: rossdale@smartchat.net.au
Premo, Liquid Sculpey

Staedtler (Pacific) Pty Ltd
PO Box 576, 1 Inman Road
Dee Why, NSW 2099
0061 2 9982 4555
Fimo

))) Canada

KJP Crafts
PO Box 5009 Merival Depot
Nepean, Ontario K2C 3H3
(613) 225-6926
E-mail: bernie.behne@attcanada.net
www.kjpcrafts.com
Premo!, Liquid Sculpey

Staedtler Mars Ltd
6 Mars Road
Etobicoke
Ontario M19V 2K1
001 416 749 3966
Fimo

))) New Zealand

Zig Zag Polymer Clay Supplies
8 Cherry Lane, Casebrook
Christ Church 8005
(+64) 3 359 2989
E-mail: petra@zigzag.co.nz
www.zigzag.co.nz
Premo!, Liquid Sculpey, Fimo, Du-Kit, cutters, powders, tool, etc.

))) United Kingdom

The Polymer Clay Pit
Meadow Rise, Wortham
Diss, Norfolk IP22 1SQ
01379 646019
Email: claypit@heaser.co.uk
www.heaser.co.uk
Premo!, Liquid Sculpey, Fimo, Creall-Therm, powders, cutters, tools, etc.

))) United States

American Art Clay Co. Inc.
4717 West Sixteenth Street
Indianapolis, IN 46222-2598
(800) 374-1600
www.amaco.com
Fimo

Clay Factory of Escondido
PO Box 460598
Escondido, CA 92046-0598
(800) 243-3466
www.clayfactoryinc.com
Premo!, Liquid Sculpey, Cernit, cutters, powders, tools, etc.

Polymer clay organizations

Please send a stamped addressed envelope when inquiring about membership.

National Polymer Clay Guild
PMB 345
1350 Beverly Road, 115
McLean, VA 22101, USA

British Polymer Clay Guild
Meadow Rise, Wortham
Diss, Norfolk 1P22 1SQ, UK

Web sites

Current information on suppliers and organizations can be found on the web site www.heaser.co.uk

Books

The following books have lots of ideas on techniques and contain some projects for the home.

Dean, Irene Semanchuk. The Weekend Crafter: Polymer Clay. Lark Books, 2000.

Ford, Steven, and Leslie Dierks. Creating with Polymer Clay. Lark Books, 1996.

Heaser, Sue. The Polymer Clay Techniques Book. North Light, 1999.

Kato, Donna. The Art of Polymer Clay. Watson Guptill Publications, 1997.

Roche, Nan. The New Clay. Flower Valley Press, 1991.

Index

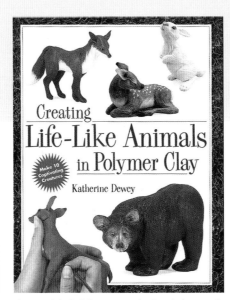

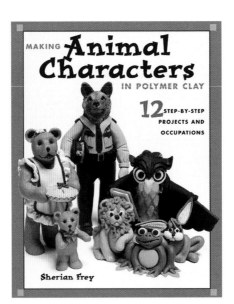
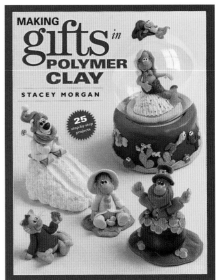